ℒ3

THE • HISTORY • OF

GOLF

THE • HISTORY • OF

GOLF

JOHN PINNER

THE
APPLE
PRESS

For my wife, Maureen — for everything good in life

A QUINTET BOOK
Published by Apple Press Ltd.
6 Blundell Street
London N7 9BH

ISBN 1-85076-113-2

This book was designed and produced by
QUINTET PUBLISHING LIMITED
6 Blundell Street
London N7 9BH

ART DIRECTOR: Peter Bridgewater
DESIGNER: Linda Henley
EDITORS: Peter Arnold, Judith Simons

Typeset in Great Britain by
Central Southern Typesetters, Eastbourne
Manufactured in Hong Kong by Regent Publishing Services Limited
Printed in Hong Kong by Leefung-Asco Printers Limited

● ACKNOWLEDGEMENTS ●

The author and publishers would like to thank: H A (Bud) Bottomley, President of
Llandrindod Wells Golf Club; Douglas Caird, *Golf World Magazine;* N (Mandy) Mitchell-Innes,
Rolls of Monmouth Golf Club; *Badminton Magazine of Sports and Pastimes* for extracts from
'Golf in Portugal' by Ethel M Skeffington (1897) and for information on golf in Japan from an
article by H E Daunt (1906). The author would also like to acknowledge his debt to
numerous books on the Royal and Ancient game without which research for this book would
have been impossible.

● PICTURE CREDITS ●

Key: *t* = top; *b* = bottom; *l* = left; *r* = right; *c* = centre.

The publishers have made every effort to identify the copyright owners of the pictures used in
this publication; they apologize for any omissions and would like to thank the following:

All-sport (UK) Ltd: pages 19 *b* (photo David Cannon); 21 *b* (photo David Cannon); 48/49;
50 *b*; 51–2; 53 (photo David Cannon); 55 *t* (photo David Cannon), *b*; 57 (photo David
Cannon); 63 (photo David Cannon); 64 *r* (photo David Cannon); 65 *l*; 66 *tl*; 67 (photo David
Cannon); 69 (photo Simon Bruty); 71 *l*; 76 *b* (photo Don Morley); 77–9 (photo David
Cannon); 81 (photo David Cannon); 82 *b*; 82/83; 83 (photo David Cannon); 84; 85 (photo
David Cannon); 86; 90 (photo David Cannon); 91; 96/97 (photo David Cannon). **Bridgeman
Art Library:** pages 9; 10/11 (courtesy of National Gallery, London). **Peter Dazeley:** pages 54;
56; 58; 62 *bl, br;* 73 *r,* 75; 76 *t,* 87; 89; 92/93; 95; 98 *t.* **Michael Hobbs Collection:** pages 7; 8;
10 *l;* 12 *t, b;* 12/13; 14 *r,* 18; 19 *t,* 20; 21 *tl, tr, c;* 22; 24–6; 27 *t,* 29; 30; 32; 37–47; 48; 49 *b;*
50 *t,* 59; 60 *tl, tr, cr, br;* 61 *tr;* 64 *tl, bl;* 65 *r,* 66 *r,* 70; 71 *tr;* 72; 73 *tl, bl;* 82 *tl;* 93 *tr, br;* 94; 97 *r,*
98 *b.* **Illustrated London News:** page 31 *t, b.* **John Pinner:** page 33. **United States Golf
Association:** pages 12 *c;* 14 *l;* 15 *t, b.* **UPI/Bettman:** pages 34–5. **Wilson Sporting Goods
Co:** pages 23; 27 *b.*

FRONT JACKET: **Illustrated London News.** BACK JACKET: **All-sport (UK) Ltd** *tl, tr;* **Michael
Hobbs Collection** *bl, c, br.*

•CONTENTS•

THE EARLY DAYS
6

THE DEVELOPMENT OF
EQUIPMENT
16

ROYALTY AND
POLITICIANS IN GOLF
28

GREAT PLAYERS OF
THE PAST AND PRESENT
36

THE MAJOR
CHAMPIONSHIPS
68

INTERNATIONAL TEAM
COMPETITIONS
80

THE GREAT COURSES
OF THE WORLD
88

MAJOR CHAMPIONSHIP
AND INTERNATIONAL
TEAM COMPETITION
RESULTS
99

THE EARLY DAYS

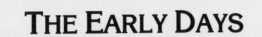

An early Dutch painting, by Aert van der Neer (1603–77),
showing golf or *kolven* being played on ice.

RIGHT AND BELOW RIGHT
Title page and front
cover of *The Art of Golf*
by Sir W G Simpson,
1887.

FAR RIGHT A painting of a
child playing golf by
Aelbert Cuyp (1620–91).

PAGES 10 & 11 (see over)
LEFT The game of *jeu de
mail* (or pall mall), 1717.

RIGHT *Golfers on Ice near
Haarlem, 1668*, Adriaen
van de Velde (1636–72).

THE

ART OF GOLF

BY

SIR W. G. SIMPSON, BART.

"SACRED TO HOPE AND PROMISE IS THE SPOT."

EDINBURGH: DAVID DOUGLAS

MDCCCLXXX

THE
ART OF GOLF

Sir W. G. Simpson, Bart.

Historians agree that it was the Scots who taught the world to play golf, but who actually invented the game is open to debate. The Scots certainly have strong claims to the title, but so too have the Dutch, French and Belgians. The sad truth is that when, where and how the game of golf came into being is a complete mystery, and will probably remain so.

What can be said is that the game has existed for at least 500 years. This we know because an Act of Parliament dated 6 March, 1457 clearly states that James II of Scotland had football and golf banned because their popularity strongly interfered with archery practice, important for the defence of the realm against the English warriors. Before this there is nothing, not even the slightest of clues, to send historians back to the archives in search of fresh evidence.

The origins of golf, therefore, are a matter of pure conjecture. This has led to many plausible theories being put forward regarding the actual birth of the game. One, more fascinating than most, comes from Sir W G Simpson in his splendid book *The Art of Golf*, wherein he suggests that a shepherd tending his flock on the links of St Andrews happened by chance to knock a pebble with his crook straight into a rabbit hole. He was challenged by a companion to repeat the stroke. The first game of golf had been played!

The Dutch game of *kolven*, a club and ball game similar to golf, which was played on ice as well as land, is supported by many old paintings. The most famous of these is *Golfers on the Ice near Haarlem, 1668*, by Adriaen van de Velde, which hangs in the National Gallery, London. However, the oldest of these paintings – a watercolour by Hendrik Avercamp – was painted in the 17th century, long after the Scottish edict. It is interesting to note that *kolven* appears in what have been claimed as the oldest references to golf in the Americas. The first of these is in the *Minutes of the Court of Fort Orange and Beverwyck, 1657*, which record that three immigrant Dutchmen were charged with playing *kolven* on a day of public prayer.

References to *chole*, the Belgian game, have been traced back to the 14th century. Played across open countryside, but with both sides playing the same ball, *chole* could quite easily have been the forerunner of golf.

There are those who think that the ancient French game called *jeu de mail* bears the closest resemblance to golf. There were four

ways of playing *jeu de mail* – *Roüet, Partie, Chicane* and *Grand Coups. Roüet* meant three- or four-ball matches. *Partie*, as the word implies, required sides of equal number. *Chicane* was similar to matchplay golf between two players. It was played in open country, along the roads, paths or lanes; each player had to play his ball from wherever it happened to lie. The winner was the player reaching a predetermined point in the least number of strokes. Even the rules bear a similarity to those of golf. Among the eight rules which governed the initial stroke, there is mention of a tee being allowed. *Grand Coups* merely meant a long-driving contest between two or more players.

In a stained-glass window in the eastern end of Gloucester Cathedral is an illustration of a figure swinging what appears to be a golf club. This was erected by Sir Thomas Bradstone during the 14th century in memory of his comrades who died at the battle of Crécy. During this same period a club and ball game called *cambuca* was popular, until in 1363 an instruction was given to sheriffs to ban all games, including *cambuca*. Although the figure in the window is today referred to as the Gloucester Golfer, it is difficult to believe that the figure depicts anything other than a man playing *cambuca*.

It is known that a game with a curved bat and a leather ball stuffed with feathers was played in Britain by the Roman soldiers. Called *paganica*, there is no evidence that it was left behind by the departing Romans. Following a peace treaty between England and Scotland in 1503, the Scots were allowed to resume their golfing activities, although it was still an offence to play on Sundays 'in tyme of sermonis'. The charge was not the playing of golf but the absence from church service. When James VI of Scotland, a keen golfer himself, succeeded to the English throne to become James I in 1603, he introduced golf to the English. It is also claimed that he was responsible for golf being started on Blackheath Common in 1608. However, the game failed to

appeal to the English and was lost until the 18th century, when the Royal Blackheath Golf Club came into existence in 1766.

In the early days of golf in Scotland, the game was played on rough common ground without any thought of class distinction, and the only class recognized was that of skill at the game. There were no greens, just crude holes cut where the surface was flattest. Golfers played together week in and week out without any thought of forming a society or club.

● THE FIRST CLUB AND ● RULES

The distinction of forming the first club goes to the Honourable Company of Edinburgh Golfers, who in 1744 were presented with a silver club by Edinburgh Council for annual competition among 'Noblemen and Gentlemen from any part of Great Britain and Ireland'. At the same time the first Rules of Golf – 13 in all – were drawn up for the inaugural competition. In 1836 the Honourable Company moved from their home at Leith to Musselburgh, and then to their present home at Muirfield in 1892.

Ten years were to lapse before the Society of St Andrews Golfers was formed. In 1834, when King William IV became the Society's patron, the title changed to the Royal and Ancient Golf Club of St Andrews, which – along with the United States Golf Association – is still the joint governing body of the game.

The establishment of these clubs, however, failed to accelerate interest in the game or extend it beyond the east coast of Scotland, perhaps more because of the expense involved than a lack of desire to take up the game. Whatever the reason, it was not until the 19th century dawned that the game began to expand, first in Scotland and England, and later in Ireland and Wales and then, with the spread of British Empire, like a prairie fire to the rest of the world.

In 1818 the Old Manchester Club was founded on Kersal Moor and became the second oldest club outside Scotland, after Royal Blackheath. The first links (seaside) course on which golf was played outside Scotland was the links of the Royal North Devon Golf Club at Westward Ho! Founded in 1864, it now houses an impressive museum of golfing memorabilia.

For nearly 50 years Royal Blackheath and Old Manchester remained the only established clubs

ABOVE Ladies playing golf at Westward Ho!, Devon, 1873.

FAR RIGHT The Crécy window in Gloucester Cathedral. The 'Gloucester Golfer' can be seen at the base of the window to the left of the picture.

RIGHT Frank Fowler's portrait of John Reid, the Scotsman who reintroduced golf to the United States in 1888.

BELOW An engraving of the awesome Cardinal bunker at Prestwick, 1889.

in England, but in India the Calcutta Club came into being in 1829, quickly followed 13 years later by the Bombay Club. Calcutta, now Royal Calcutta, is the oldest club in the world outside Britain. The first Continental club was formed at Pau, in southern France, in 1856. Golf had earlier been introduced to this region in 1814, when officers of the Duke of Wellington's army were stationed at Pau after the battle of Orthez. Amazingly, they had their clubs with them, and laid out a temporary course on the plain of Billère. They must have enjoyed the experience, because many years later they returned to the area to take a holiday.

In 1851 the west coast of Scotland gained its first golf course when the inhabitants of Prestwick showed a lively interest in the game. The first British Open Championship was staged there in 1860.

Australia received its first taste of golf in 1871 with the opening of the Adelaide Club, while in 1885 the Cape Club, in South Africa, was formed. Both these clubs now carry the Royal prefix.

● GOLF IN THE UNITED ●
STATES

For some unexplained reason golf failed to gain a foothold in the United States when it was first tried out there in the 18th century. There is much evidence that golf courses were laid out at Charleston, South Carolina, in 1786 and at Savannah, Georgia, in 1795. But these quickly disappeared from the scene, and it was in Canada that golf took its first firm roots in North America. The oldest club is Royal Montreal, formed in the autumn of 1873, and followed two years later by the Quebec Club, and in 1876 by Toronto.

Surprisingly, when golf returned to stay in the United States, in 1888, it was from small beginnings. A Scotsman (it had to be a Scot), John Reid, from Dunfermline, hearing that a close friend, Robert Lockhart, was planning a trip to Britain, asked him to bring back some balls and clubs. Lockhart duly obliged by purchasing from the shop of Old Tom Morris in St Andrews (where else?) a set of six golf clubs and two dozen balls. Eventually a rough patch of land across Lake Avenue from Reid's home in Yonkers, New York, was eagerly converted into three holes. From that day, 22 February, 1888, golf was in full swing, literally, in the United States.

Afterwards Reid and four friends, John Upham, Harry Holbrook, Kingman Putnam and Henry O Tallnadge obtained a 30-acre site and turned it into a six-hole course. On 14 November, 1888, they formed the St Andrews Club of Yonkers, with John Reid as its first president. To mark the historic occasion they drank a toast, not to John Reid, but to Robert Lockhart, for producing the vital equipment which launched the resurrection of golf in the United States. They earned the immortal nickname The Apple Tree Gang when four years later they moved their course to a large apple orchard. Since their new course lacked a clubhouse, they made a habit of hanging jugs of liquid refreshment on a large apple tree which bordered the home hole.

In no time at all golf began to capture the hearts of Americans everywhere, and soon became a national pastime. There is an amusing tailpiece to this important piece of American sporting history. Shortly after returning from Britain with the famous clubs and balls, Mr Lockhart was arresting for hitting a golf ball about in Central Park! A little later, in 1891, the Shinnecock Hills Golf Club on Long Island was founded. It takes a prominent place in the chronicles of American golf by virtue of becoming the first incorporated club in the United States and also for having built the first clubhouse deemed necessary to cater for its 44 members.

Charles Blair Macdonald, who had expertly learned the game while a student at St Andrews University, Scotland, achieved the honour of designing and building the United States' first 18-hole course when he laid out the Chicago Golf Club course at Wheaton, Illinois, in 1893. In later life he created the National Links on Long Island, reproducing the finest holes he had played during his time in Britain. He gained further fame in 1895, when he became the United States' first National Amateur Champion by defeating Charles Sands by the wide margin of 12 and 11 at Newport, Rhode Island. The following day – also at Newport – saw the first Open Championship of the United States. It was won by a young Englishman, Horace Rawlins, who had recently arrived in the United States to take up the assistant professional post at Newport Golf Club. Willie Dunn, a Scottish professional who had earlier been hired to plan the

Shinnecock course, was the runner-up.

Both these historic tournaments took place as a direct result of the formation in December 1894 of the United States Golf Association, which remains to this day the sport's national governing body.

Never slow in doing things, the Americans, by the turn of the century, had opened over 1,000 golf clubs. Knowing a good thing when they saw it, the Scottish professionals migrated to the United States in droves to earn good money from teaching the wonderful new game. From a humble three-hole course to more clubs than the rest of the world in just 12 years is, indeed, an extraordinary happening in the history of an extraordinary pastime.

In the same year as John Reid and his friends were laying out their small course at Yonkers, the Principality of Wales gained its first recognized golf course at the seaside town of Tenby. Two others – at Pontnewydd and Borth – lay claim to having been in existence at least a decade before Tenby, but no definite record that either of these clubs precede Tenby has actually been discovered.

Golf, like a great new religion, continued to sweep the globe. Scottish officers stationed at the Curragh, Ireland, while waiting to go to the Crimean War, started what later became the Royal Curragh Golf Club, and in 1881 the Royal Belfast Club was born.

In 1889 when six British enthusiasts laid out a nine-hole links in the Portuguese fishing village of Espinho, situated some ten miles south of Oporto, they reckoned without one rather serious hazard. During the summer months of July and August – the great bull-fighting season – the bulls used in the arena were put out to grass in the area during the week prior to being

driven into Oporto for the Saturday night spectacle. They made a nasty habit of tearing up the flags, and sometimes the greens. Hidden by the sand dunes, they often appeared unexpectedly. With one eye on the ball and the other on the bull, it is little wonder that golfers scored highly during this period!

Another humorous tale emerging from this course concerns the young sons of the local sardine fishermen. Frequently employed on the links as caddies, they prided themselves on knowing the name of every club in English. One was overheard telling another he had learnt to

ABOVE LEFT Early golfers at St Andrews, Yonkers, New York.

ABOVE A portrait of William Innes, Captain of Blackheath, and his caddie, by Lemuel Abbott (1760–1803).

count the strokes in English, having listened carefully to the gentleman for whom he was carrying. He then proceeded to teach the others – 'one, two, three, four, five, six, damn, eight, damn' – and then said he could not understand why the English used the same word to mean seven and nine, and why it should be used with greater emphasis than the others.

What irresistable force prompted Arthur Groom into creating Japan's first course on the summit of Mount Rokko, Kobe, in 1903 is difficult to comprehend. A merchant with a thriving business of 30-years standing in the seaport town of Kobe, he was already a very busy man and he had never played golf in his life before opening his course. What a place to choose to build a golf course: 3,000 ft (900 m) above sea level! In those days of primitive transport it took over two tortuous hours to reach the top of Mount Rokko from Kobe. Imagine the journey: half-an-hour by rickshaw to the entrance of the Cascade Valley, a 60-minute climb by foot through to the Gap before an even stiffer climb to the long stretch of flat at the top. Horse riding was possible, but extremely dangerous. Those willing to take the risk could be carried up the slopes by coolies in a *kago*, a type of basket slung on a pole. All this for a quiet game of golf. It was hardly surprising that upon arrival the golfers opted to stay the whole weekend at the clubhouse.

Mr Groom sought the advice of Messrs Adamson and Mcmurtrie, both of whom had learnt the game in their boyhood in Scotland before moving to Japan, to help him construct the original four holes. The course was finally extended to 18 holes in 1904, by which time the membership numbered over 200 – mostly British but with a sprinkling of Germans and Japanese. The first honorary secretary of the Kobe Golf Club was Arthur H Groom himself. What a remarkable man, and what a remarkable golf course.

As a result of the English merchant's enterprise other courses began to materialize inside the empire. Six holes were built on the sand flats of Yokoya, a small village 30 minutes from Kobe on the road to Osaka, and in 1906 British settlers in Yokohama formed the first links in eastern Japan, at Negishi. This was followed in 1914 by the Tokyo Club, built by the Japanese. China, Hong Kong and other countries in the Far East quickly followed suit, and golf had encircled the world.

LEFT An early photograph of Shinnecock Hills Golf Club, New York.

BELOW Charles Blair Macdonald, the first winner of the United States Amateur Championship in 1895.

THE DEVELOPMENT OF EQUIPMENT

A persimmon-headed wood club.

In ancient times any club and ball game simply meant just that – one club and one ball – and golf was no exception. The club would have been a suitably selected branch of a tree, probably thornwood or beech, cut to an acceptable size and crudely fashioned into a curved stick. The ball would be shaped from hardwood or, as used by the Romans for *paganica*, made from leather and stuffed with feathers. If either of these primitive implements needed replacing, the job would have been done by the player himself.

THE EMERGENCE OF CLUBMAKERS

Although no evidence exists before the early part of the 17th century that clubmaking had become a profession, it is obvious that before this, as the game progressed and became popular among the gentry, craftsmen like carpenters and bowmakers would turn their skills toward producing golf clubs as a means of making a better living.

The first authentic record of a recognized clubmaker appears in 1603 when William Mayne, a maker of bows and arrows, was appointed to the court of James I of England to make, among other things, clubs for the golf-loving King and his courtiers. The only earlier reference to golf clubs being specially made dates from exactly a century before, when James IV of Scotland requested his Lord High Treasurer to purchase a supply from a bowmaker in Perth. No specimens from these periods survive, so we have no knowledge of the methods or standard of workmanship of these early craftsmen.

After Mayne, we have to go to the late 1600s before discovering two more named clubmakers – Andrew Dickson and Henry Mill of Leith and St Andrews, respectively. In addition to being a celebrated clubmaker, Dickson often acted as a caddie to James II at Leith. He is also the Dickson referred to in the immortal 1743 poem *The Goff*, by Thomas Matheson:

> Of finest ash, Castalio's shaft was made;
> Pondrous with lead and fenced with horn
>   the head,
> The work of Dickson who in Letha dwells
> And in the art of making clubs excels.

An original copy of this heroic-comical poem in

three cantos was sold at auction by Phillips of Chester, England, in 1985 for the staggering sum of £17,000.

The poem contains a clue as to how the clubs were made. Most of the shafts were of ash or hazel to give the club 'whip', and the back of the head had a shallow hollow which was filled with lead for extra weight and balance. On the face an insert of leather, horn or bone was often attached as a prevention against damage. The heads were fashioned from beech, holly, dogwood or blackthorn; most of the fruit-woods – plum, pear and apple – were also tried. The usual method of joining the shaft to the head was to splice the specially tapered ends together with glue, then firmly bind them with pitched twine to strengthen the join. This method became known as 'scare-headed', scare being derived from the word 'scarf' (an overlapping join). Clubs continued to be made this way until the latter part of the 19th century, when the socket-head method was invented. A scare-headed club bearing the stamp of a famous clubmaker can fetch a tidy sum at auction today.

A set of these wooden clubs, believed to have been crafted by either Dickson or Mill, was found along with two iron-headed clubs behind a false wall in an old dwelling at Hull, in northern England, during renovations in 1889. Unfortunately, the large stamp on each of the wooden clubs is illegible through wear, leaving the maker's identity a matter of conjecture. How-

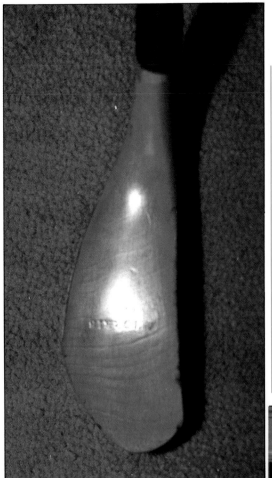

ever, among documents found with the now priceless clubs was a newspaper dated 1741 establishing them at a much earlier date than the paper. They were eventually purchased by Adam Wood, captain of the Troon Club for five years from 1893, and as the oldest extant clubs are preserved in the Big Room of the clubhouse at Troon.

No records have come to light of other clubmakers immediately following Dickson and Mill, and we have to wait until the Georgian era before finding the name of Simon Cossar of Leith, who was appointed clubmaker to the Honourable Company of Gentlemen Golfers in the middle of the 18th century. Three fine examples of his work – two wooden clubs and a putting cleek from about 1760 – can be seen in the Royal and Ancient Club of St Andrews museum.

In the wake of Cossar came notable clubmakers such as the McEwens, Philp, Wilson, Carrick and White. The last three specialized in

LEFT A scared-head driver, made by Tom Morris senior and stamped with his name.

RIGHT This rare collection of feather balls and feather ball-making implements includes: two awls with chest braces, a leather ball-holder, two short awls, two wooden feather-stuffers and a set of callipers. The Royal and Ancient Trophy Room, St Andrews, Scotland.

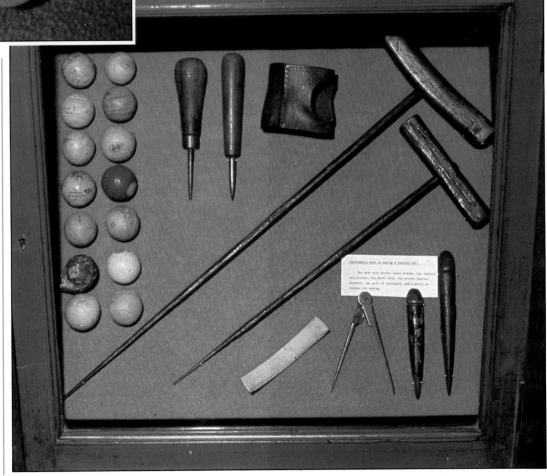

ABOVE Horace Hutchinson, a champion golfer and a prolific sports writer, 1896.

clubmaking family, practising their craft for well over a century. James, formerly a wheelwright, founded the business in 1770 at Leith. A son, Peter, born in 1781, followed his father into the business and later married the daughter of Douglas Gourlay of Musselburgh, a celebrated ballmaker of the period, thus linking two of the most important names in the development of golf equipment. Their son Douglas succeeded to the business and became a true master of the craft. His wooden clubs, along with those of Hugh Philp, are now much sought after by collectors of golf antiquities, who regard their works as the Chippendales of the golfing world.

Born in 1782, Hugh Philp started his working life as a carpenter but turned his attention to making golf clubs. He rapidly gained a reputation for making quality clubs that were in a special class of their own. Such was his success that in 1819 he was appointed official clubmaker to the Society of St Andrews Golfers. As often happens today with top-quality goods, many attempts were made to imitate his work. For a short time after his death in 1856, a couple of unscrupulous characters gained illegal possession of his stampmarker. However, although bearing the name of Philp, the imitations were easily recognizable as fakes by their beech heads and by their inferior quality (Philp invariably used pear, apple or thorn in his heads, and his clubs were more delicately balanced). Philp was described by many as the prince of clubmakers, and replicas of his work are being produced to this day by a number of club professionals who make a steady income from the practice. Examples of Philp's work can be seen at the Royal and Ancient Club of St Andrews, where a complete set of his woods is on display in the Trophy Room.

Most of the clubs of this period, including the putter, had wooden heads, and a set usually consisted of six or seven, with maybe a track iron added. Strange as it may seem today, a bag with which to carry the clubs was still to be invented (the first golf bag appeared about 1880). Clubs were simply carried in the crook of the arm, as if they were a bundle of garden implements. Even the medieval bowmen used a quiver to carry their arrows and the warrior a scabbard for his sword, so why the early golfer preferred not to use a container of sorts for his clubs is a mystery.

Regarding the almost total absence of iron-headed clubs in the early days, Horace

the making of cleeks (iron-headed clubs) and the 'Carrick' cleek in particular was much in demand by virtue of its perfect balance and durability. A popular cleek at this time was the track iron, its lofted head usually made of iron although there are examples in gun-metal or bronze (used to prevent rusting). The track iron derived its name from the fact that up to about 1860 it was specially used to extricate the ball out of cart tracks, then frequently found on the Scottish links as a result of the townspeople having public right of way to cart sand, seaweed, flotsam and jetsam across the course. This club was the forerunner of the modern wedge and sand iron.

The McEwens were a famous, long-standing

FAR LEFT A fine example of a track, or rut, iron.

LEFT An early American advertisement for golf equipment. The Boston firm of Wright & Ditson began marketing clubs c 1895.

BELOW Original feather balls are now valuable items, much sought after by golf collectors.

BOTTOM This collection of rare golfing memorabilia includes: old rule books, early gutty balls and a beautiful set of miniature wooden clubs, made by Willie Auchterlonie, the 1893 Open champion. Royal and Ancient Trophy Room, St Andrews.

Hutchinson – a champion golfer and prolific golf writer in his day – tells a delightful story in the Lonsdale Library book, *The Game of Golf*, on how his knowledge of golf history saved a friend a considerable amount of money. Contemplating buying a golfing picture by Johann Zoffany, the friend asked Hutchinson to take a look at it. The picture showed a gentleman in the costume of the period (late 18th century) holding a club in the crook of his arm. At his feet knelt a young caddie, teeing up a ball, while a set of clubs lay on the ground, four with wooden heads and four with iron. Explaining to his friend that the use of an equal proportion of iron and wooden clubs was most unusual for Zoffany's period, Hutchinson said it loud enough to be overhead by the picture dealer. Microscopic examination by the dealer later clearly showed that the club under the gentleman's arm was originally a walking-cane – the kneeling boy, the ball and the clubs on the ground had all been added later by a faker! Collectors of golf antiques take note.

As the years rolled on and the game grew popular worldwide, the demand for clubs saw many more clubmakers appearing on the scene. Persimmon, there being a plentiful supply from the United States, replaced other wood for the making of heads, while hickory was found to be best for the shafts. With the introduction of the gutta-percha ball, iron clubs of varying loft became an important part of the golfer's armoury, giving blacksmiths a chance to show their skills.

With the dawning of the 20th century, experiments with steel-shafted clubs were being carried out but, reluctant to break with tradition, the Royal and Ancient Club banned the use of such clubs. The ban continued in Britain until 1929, five years after steel shafts had been judged legal in America by the United States Golf Association. It is believed that Thomas Horsburgh of Edinburgh first tried such clubs in the 1890s, but failed to make progress because of the eventual ban.

Today steel continues to be the primary material for shafts, but graphite and carbon-fibre shafts are gradually beginning to make their mark. Although it sounds contradictory, metal-headed woods are also becoming popular. The only wooden-shafted clubs in use today are putters – relics of the past or reproductions. Today the manufacturing of clubs, like other sports equipment, is big business and millions of clubs are mass-produced each year.

● THE DEVELOPMENT OF THE BALL ●

We know that the Romans used a ball made from a leather bag stuffed with feathers when playing *paganica*, but whether this type of ball remained in existence until it was used by Scots golfers in the 17th century is doubtful. There is some indication that wooden balls were used by the early golfers, but the earliest modern reference to makers of the feather ball is the granting of a monopoly in 1618 by James VI of Scotland (James I of England) to James Melvill and his associate for a period of 21 years. He also decreed that the price of the ball was not to exceed a certain limit and each ball was to be marked with the maker's stamp; all balls made within the kingdom marked otherwise were to be confiscated.

The making of a 'feathery', as it became commonly known, called for much patience. The leather was of untanned bull's hide that was cut into two round pieces for the ends and a narrow strip for the middle, then softened and firmly sown together, leaving a small hole through which to stuff the feathers. To give the ball a smooth finish the leather was turned inside out so that the rough seams were hidden inside. The leather casing was then placed in a cup-shaped stand and the boiled feathers – as many as would fill a top hat – were stuffed through the hole with the aid of a metal 'pusher'. Inserting the feathers was a slow and laborious operation and the inhaling of small particles from the feathers often caused respiratory problems. A ballmaker could feel well satisfied if he produced three featheries in a full working day.

Distances achieved with the feathery depended on weather conditions. When dry it could be struck on average about 180 yards (165 m), when wet about 150 yards (135 m). It is said that a Swiss tutor at St Andrews University, one Simon Messieux, once hit a wind-assisted feathery more than 350 yards (320 m) on the Old Course. For this distance to be reached by a feathery, we must assume the strength of the wind was near gale force.

After Melvill's 21-year monopoly ended, other ballmakers began to emerge. John Dickson of Leith, who is assumed to be the son of Andrew Dickson the clubmaker mentioned earlier, was granted a licence by the town council of Aber-

LEFT A modern metal-headed wood.

BELOW LEFT A pair of Schenectady putters made in the United States at the turn of the century. This type of club, of a revolutionary centre-shafted design, was used by Walter Travis to win the 1904 British Amateur Championship. Judging it 'untraditional', the Royal and Ancient Club of St Andrews banned it a few years later.

BELOW An up-to-the-minute wood and iron, marketed by Wilson.

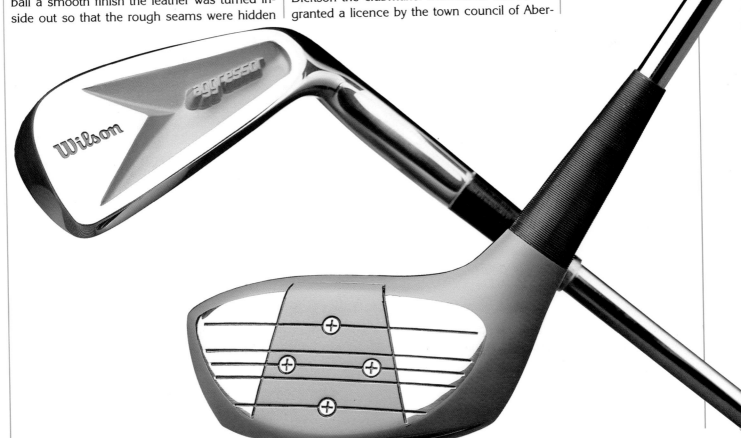

deen in 1642 to make balls within the borough. By the middle of the 18th century the making of the feathery had become a profitable business. About this time the family firm Gourlay of Bruntsfield and Musselburgh was founded by Douglas Gourlay of Leith. The Gourlay ball was to last for a century with a reputation that was second to none. Its fame was such that it became much praised in poetry and song by the bards of that time. Made to perfection, it commanded a high price.

In 1815 Allan Robertson was born. He was destined to become the first great professional golfer, but first he joined the family business and soon rivalled the Gourlays in the art of making feather balls. In his shop at St Andrews, in 1840, he and his assistant Tom Morris senior (also to become a famous professional) turned out 1,021 balls between them. In 1844 they produced 2,456 and, naturally, they were delighted with their progress. Little did they realize that looming on the horizon was a revolutionary new ball made from gutta-percha which was soon to make the feathery obsolete.

● THE GUTTA-PERCHA BALL ●

During the second half of the 19th century ballmakers and golfers rejoiced when it was discovered that the reddish-brown, horn-like substance of the inspissated juice of the Malaysian gutta-percha tree made perfectly good golf balls. Ballmakers were pleased because they were freed from the daily tedious grind of turning out feather balls, and golfers because the new ball, quickly and easily made, cost but a fraction of the feathery.

The 'gutty', as it inevitably became called, was first made in 1848 by a clergyman from St Andrews, the Reverend Robert Adam Paterson, who hit upon the idea after receiving from India a marble statue of Vishna (now in St Andrews University) which was wrapped in a protective padding of gutta-percha. Knowing that gutta-percha could be softened by heat and subsequently mould-

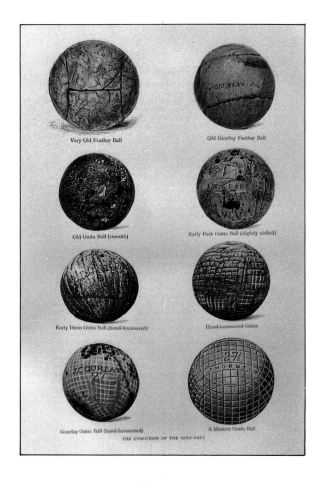

Very Old Feather Ball

Old Gourlay Feather Ball

Old Gutta Ball (smooth)

Early Park Gutta Ball (slightly nicked)

Early Dunn Gutta Ball (hand-hammered)

Hand-hammered Gutta

Gourlay Gutta Ball (hand-hammered)

A Modern Gutta Ball

THE EVOLUTION OF THE GOLF-BALL

ed by hand, he experimented with the substance and came up with a ball which set rock-hard when cooled. Flushed with success he patented the ball under the name 'Paterson's Patent'. The ball, however, was not an instant success. Much too smooth, it had a tendency to duck in flight. It was often remarked upon that the gutty flew better at the end of the round than it did at the beginning. It did not take long for someone to realize its performance improved after it had been cut about a bit by the cleeks. It was normal practice at the finish of a round for the ball to be soaked in hot water until soft, and the offending cuts to be erased. Used again, it behaved as before – erratic at first, becoming better as play progressed.

An experiment was carried out in which a newly moulded ball was scored all over with the sharp end of a saddler's hammer. It proved highly successful, and the demise of the feather ball was inevitable.

Some ballmakers, however, were dismayed by the advent of the gutty. They saw it as a threat to their continuing prosperity. Allan Robertson refused to have anything to do with the new ball – he would not play with it, make it or sell it in his shop. Such was his hatred of it that he bought all the old specimens that were offered him by the ball-finders who scratched a living searching for lost balls in the St Andrews rough, and set them alight without regard to the obnoxious smell the fire created. His stubbornness continuing, he

TOP Walter Travis watching the ball intently during the 1904 British Amateur Championship at Sandwich.

ABOVE Sandy Herd lining up for a shot at St Andrews, c 1899. (Notice the extra-wide stance.)

ABOVE RIGHT Lee Trevino using a four-wheeled caddie car.

RIGHT A modern professional's golf bag.

eventually lost the services of Tom Morris. Morris had promised Robertson he would never play with the gutty, but in a moment of forgetfulness he borrowed a gutty from a partner to give it a try during a friendly round over the St Andrews links. Robertson heard about this, and was furious. This resulted in Tom Morris leaving Robertson and going into business on his own in a shop overlooking the Old Course at St Andrews – the same shop Robert Lockhart was to visit 40 years later in order to purchase for his friend John Reid the balls and clubs which would resurrect golf in the United States.

As time went by Robertson grew to realize he could make as much, if not more, from selling the gutty because, being cheaper, it was being bought by people with small incomes who were now taking up the game. As they also needed to buy clubs, the arrival of the gutty eventually turned out to be a godsend for the trade. John Gourlay, who had succeeded to the head of the famous family ballmaking firm, was also reluctant to change, but upon observing that the gutty was accurate in flight, kept a good line to the hole when putted and was not prone to bursting in mid-air like the feathery, he knew that the days of the feathery were numbered, and proved more astute than Robertson by making sure that all outstanding orders for the feathery were despatched in double quick time.

Eventually, iron moulds were invented, but on leaving the mould the ball still had to be scored with a hammer. Later the moulds were improved to indent each ball automatically.

Except for a short period in the 1890s when a ball consisting of a mixture of rubber, cork and metal filings called the 'Eclipse' was introduced (without much success), the gutta-percha ball reigned supreme for almost 55 years, until it was superseded by the Haskell ball in 1903.

● THE HASKELL BALL ●

The introduction of the Haskell rubber-cored ball brought about an even greater interest in the game, especially in the United States. The brainchild of an American dentist, Dr Coburn Haskell, of Cleveland, Ohio, the ball was composed of strips of elastic wound tightly round a liquid-filled rubber core, with a casing of gutta-percha added. Dr Haskell invented the ball in 1899 and American golfers began to take it seriously in 1901, when Walter Travis, an Australian who had made his home in America, won the United States Amateur Championship using the Haskell ball.

At first the British gave the new ball a cool reception. Even when Charles Hutchings, at the age of 53, beat Sidney Fry in the 1902 final of the British Amateur Championship at Hoylake, with both finalists using the Haskell ball, it was still looked upon with suspicion by the majority of British golfers. The British professionals, and there were quite a few of them by this time, declared openly that they would continue to play with the gutty in all their matches. But one among them was to have second thoughts. On the eve of the 1902 British Open Championship, also at Hoylake, Alex Herd used a Haskell, purely out of curiosity, during a practice round. Taking a liking to the ball he took a gamble by deciding to use the Haskell in the Championship; to everyone's amazement, he won the coveted title with a stroke to spare. As the news spread of Herd's success with the new ball, golfers everywhere wanted to play with the Haskell. The gutty was dead. Long live the Haskell!

The success of the Haskell was due largely to its behaviour when struck. It was easy to raise from the ground, it travelled much further and, even when mis-hit, usually travelled a respectable distance. People found the game much easier to play and more and more came forward to swell the ranks. Modern techniques have brought about subsequent improvements to the golf ball, which have resulted in its travelling even further than previously.

In an effort to prevent big hitters making a mockery of the shorter courses, the twin governing bodies, the R and A and the USGA, have placed a velocity restriction on the ball which at present is limited to 250 ft (76 m) per second, with a 2 percent tolerance. In addition, in the United States and all countries using USGA rules, the ball must measure at least 1.68 in (42.67 mm) in diameter and not be heavier than 1.62 oz (45.93 g). In Britain and the rest of the world, golfers playing in ordinary club competitions have the option of playing the 1.68 in (42.67 mm) ball or the smaller 1.62 in (41.15 mm) ball which must weigh the same as the larger ball, 1.62 oz (45.93 g). However, it is now compulsory to use the big ball in all professional tournaments and all important amateur events at national, state and county levels.

Most balls now have a covering of the more durable balata or surlyn in preference to gutta-percha, and the two-piece ball with its even tougher synthetic cover and solid core is becoming increasingly popular.

To say that the ball has played its part in the development of golf would be an understatement. In a little over 50 years these two ingenious men from opposite sides of the Atlantic did more to revolutionize golf than anybody else centuries before. Each of these men in turn was responsible for more people becoming golfers, thus setting in motion a chain reaction. More courses had to be constructed to accommodate them, stronger golf clubs had to be found to withstand the hardness of the balls and iron-headed clubs with varying degrees of loft became necessary. With many more clubs to carry, the golf bag finally came into being and new rules had to be introduced.

As well as the rule regarding the size and weight of the ball mentioned earlier, the twin governing bodies found it necessary to restrict to 14 the number of clubs an individual may carry in a recognized competition. Before this rule was imposed some players were carrying more than double this number, each devised by a manufacturer to make the game easier.

With the numbers of players multiplying there was, of course, a shortage of caddies. This brought about the development of the golf trolley. Manually operated when first introduced, there are now many makes of battery-operated trolleys on the market and many players, especially in Britain, use this type of trolley. Even more advanced is the four-wheeled buggy or cart or caddie-car, powered by a small petrol engine or powerful sets of batteries. These vehicles are designed to carry not only two sets of clubs but also the players to whom they belong. Although much used in the United States, elsewhere they are looked upon as more of a luxury than a necessity, except when used by disabled golfers. Another version of the golf cart or caddie-car, recently introduced, has three wheels and caters to the individual golfer.

Unlike their predecessors, golfers today wear shoes with specially moulded or metal-spiked soles, colourful casual clothing, sun visors and gloves. Wet-weather waterproof suits and large umbrellas help players stay dry. Plastic tees, hand towels, ball cleaners, distance charts, rule books, scorecards and practice aids are all very much taken for granted. How different to the golfer in those far-off days with his single club and wooden ball!

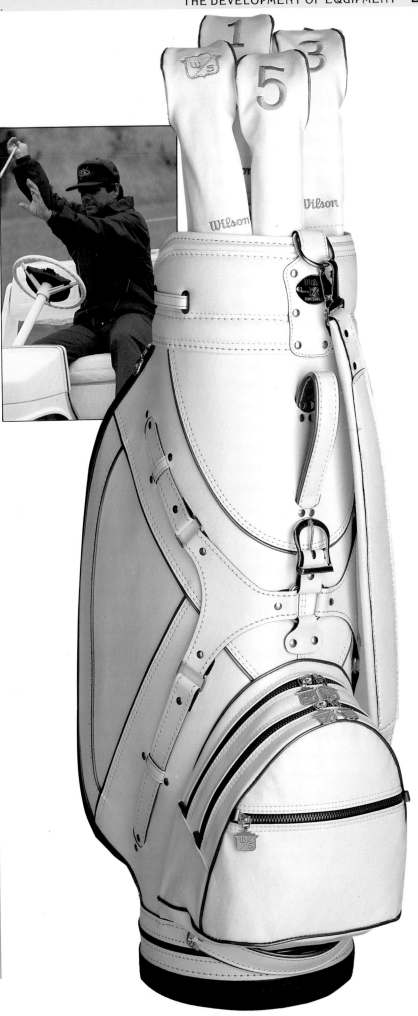

ROYALTY
AND POLITICIANS IN GOLF

A famous quintet: Bobby Jones, the Duchess of Windsor,
Walter Hagen, the Duke of Windsor and Tommy
Armour.

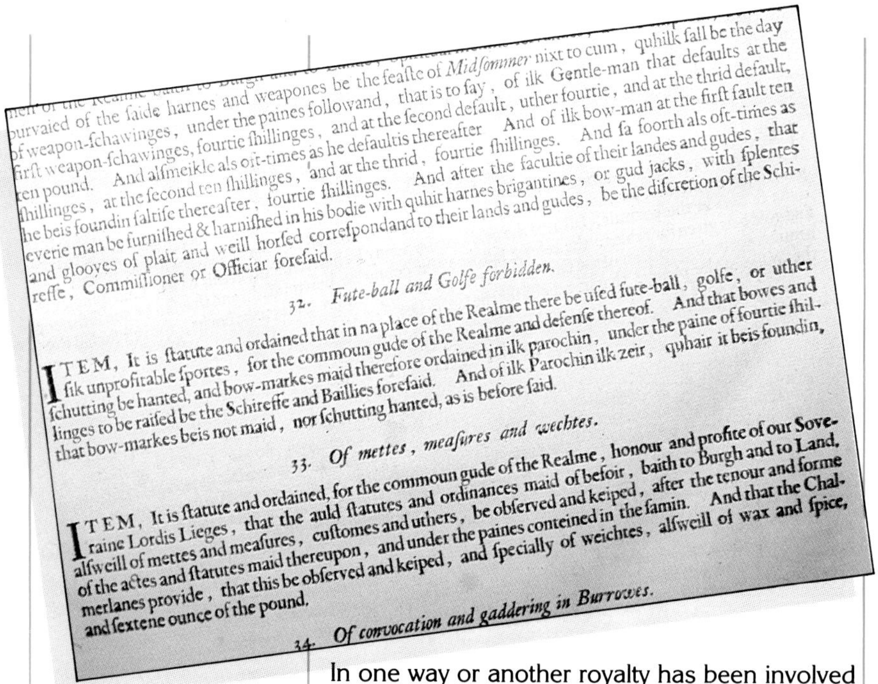
purvaied of the ſaide harnes and weapones be the feaſte of *Midſommer* nixt to cum, quhilk ſall be the day of weapon-ſchawinges, under the paines followand, that is to ſay, of ilk Gentle-man that defaults at the firſt weapon-ſchawinges, fourtie ſhillinges, and at the ſecond default, uther fourtie, and at the thrid default, ten pound. And alſmeikle als oft-times as he defaultis thereafter And of ilk bow-man at the firſt fault ten ſhillinges, at the ſecond ten ſhillinges, and at the thrid, fourtie ſhillinges. And ſa foorth als oft-times as he beis foundin faltiſe thereafter, fourtie ſhillinges. And after the facultie of their landes and gudes, that everie man be furniſhed & harniſhed in his bodie with quhit harnes brigantines, or gud jacks, with ſplentes and glooyes of plait and weill horſed correſpondand to their lands and gudes, be the diſcretion of the Schireffe, Commiſſioner or Officiar foreſaid.

32. *Fute-ball and Golfe forbidden.*

ITEM, It is ſtatute and ordained that in na place of the Realme there be uſed fute-ball, golfe, or uther ſik unprofitable ſportes, for the commoun gude of the Realme and defenſe thereof. And that bowes and ſchutting be hanted, and bow-markes maid therefore ordained in ilk parochin, under the paine of fourtie ſhillinges to be raiſed be the Schireffe and Baillies foreſaid. And of ilk Parochin ilk zeir, quhair it beis foundin, that bow-markes beis not maid, nor ſchutting hanted, as is before ſaid.

33. *Of mettes, meaſures and wechtes.*

ITEM, It is ſtatute and ordained, for the commoun gude of the Realme, honour and profite of our Soveraine Lordis Lieges, that the auld ſtatutes and ordinances maid of befoir, baith to Burgh and to Land, alſweill of mettes and meaſures, cuſtomes and uthers, be obſerved and keiped, after the tenour and forme of the actes and ſtatutes maid thereupon, and under the paines conteined in the ſamin. And that the Chalmerlanes provide, that this be obſerved and keiped, and ſpecially of weichtes, alſweill of wax and ſpice, and ſextene ounce of the pound.

34. *Of convocation and gaddering in Burrowes.*

ABOVE Golf was obviously a popular pastime in 15th-century Scotland – so popular, in fact, that men of military age were found to be neglecting their compulsory archery practice. In 1491 James IV of Scotland redressed the situation by issuing an act banning golf and other 'unprofitable' sports.

In one way or another royalty has been involved with golf for over five centuries. The earliest mention we have of a monarch in connection with the game is, of course, James II of Scotland, to whom historians shall be forever grateful for providing the first written proof of the existence of golf in medieval times with his famous edict of 1457.

In 1471 James III repeated the edict and in 1491 James IV, despite his fondness for golf, saw fit to issue a similar act. Whether James IV was actually the first royal to play golf we know not. However, his is the first name recorded as having done so. Following his lifting of the ban in 1503 – repealed because his marriage to Princess Margaret, daughter of Henry VII of England, brought peace to the two countries – the Lord High Treasurer's accounts show that the King drew a sum to settle a golfing debt with the Earl of Bothwell, and to pay for the clubs and balls that had failed him.

A few years later, in 1506, two more items in the accounts tell us that more clubs and balls were purchased by the golfing monarch. But little time remained for him to pursue his favourite pastime, for he fell at the Battle of Flodden in 1515, going to war against his brother-in-law Henry VIII.

Two years before this tragic event there is evidence of Queen Catherine of Aragon, first wife of King Henry VIII, finding comfort in golf, while her husband was engaged in more worldly pursuits. In a letter to Cardinal Wolsey she regretted that she would not be hearing often from her husband, but that his subjects would be glad to hear that 'thank God she would be busy with golfe for her heart was very good to it'.

After James IV, there followed a long line of golfing Stuarts. James V played many times at Gosford, in East Lothian, on a course privately owned by the Earl of Wemyss. Mary Queen of Scots, the ill-fated daughter of James V, much enjoyed playing golf on the links of St Andrews, and is said to have played golf in fields alongside Seton House only a few days after the murder of her husband, Lord Darnley, who was found strangled at Kirk-o'-Field, outside Edinburgh, in February 1567. If Queen Elizabeth I, like Mary, had been a keen golfer maybe the two would have settled their differences over a round of golf rather than Mary having to lose her head in February 1587 at Fotheringay Castle.

James IV's great grandson, James VI, the future James I of England, acquired his golfing skills at North Inch, Perth, and when he succeeded Elizabeth to the throne of England in 1603 he took golf south into England with him and his court. Both his sons, Prince Charles and Henry, Prince of Wales, who died of a fever in 1612 before reaching manhood, were ardent golfers. Charles, who ascended the English throne as Charles I, was halfway through a round of golf at Leith when he received news of the Irish Rebellion. Following the example of Sir Francis Drake, who completed his game of bowls before dealing with the Spanish Armada, Charles did likewise and played on. Four years later, in 1645, having been captured by the Scottish army at Newcastle, Charles was permitted to play golf on the Shield field outside the walls of the castle where he was imprisoned.

Charles II also played golf, but nothing is known of his dedication to the game. However, James II of England, when Duke of York and domiciled in Scotland as Lord High Commissioner on the order of his brother Charles II in 1681, often found time to play golf on Leith links, Edinburgh. It was there that he took part in what can loosely be called the first international golf match. Two English noblemen provoked the Duke into an argument by claiming that the game was of English origin rather than Scottish. To settle the dispute the English pair suggested a foursome match be played for a large wager between themselves and the Duke with any Scotsman of his choice as his partner. The Duke wisely chose for his partner John Paterson, a shoemaker who was the local cham-

tested at the annual autumn meeting. Following his death a few weeks later, his widow, Queen Adelaide, consented to become patron and presented a medal inscribed with her name, with the request that it be worn by the captain on all public occasions. Since that time successive captains have carried on the tradition of wearing the Queen Adelaide Medal.

Queen Victoria, who was to reign supreme over the British Empire for 64 years, also became patron of the Royal and Ancient Club. Her eldest son, Edward Prince of Wales, the future Edward VII, showed a deep interest in the game when he consented to be Captain of the R and A in 1863. A measure of his interest can be taken from the fact that during his reign he had a golf course laid out for himself in the Home Park at Windsor. Visitors to Windsor are able to spot part of the course, which comes up to the rear of

LEFT This detail of a drawing by A Forestier records the tradition that, while in St Andrews in 1563, Mary Queen of Scots enjoyed a round of golf on the local links.

BELOW King Edward VII of England photographed on the links during a visit to Biarritz in 1908.

pion. The Duke and the shoemaker won handsomely with holes to spare, and the Duke, overjoyed at their victory, presented Paterson with half of the wager he had won. There being no amateur code to worry about in those days, Paterson gladly accepted the money and promptly invested it by building himself a large house in Edinburgh.

With the decline of the Stuarts, golf fell out of favour with royalty. Indeed, royal involvement lay dormant until 1833, when William IV granted permission for the Perth Golfing Society to carry the 'Royal' prefix – thus creating the first 'Royal' golf club. A year later he became patron of the St Andrews Golfing Society, and bestowed the title of The Royal and Ancient Golf Club of St Andrews on the illustrious society. Afterward, in 1837, he presented the club with the Gold Medal for a yearly competition which is still being con-

ABOVE Arthur James Balfour (far right), the first British prime minister to become addicted to golf.

Windsor Castle. In 1876 Prince Leopold, the last of Victoria's sons, followed in his brother's footsteps by also becoming Captain of the Royal and Ancient Club, and in the same year their brother Arthur, the Duke of Connaught, became Honorary President of the Musselburgh Golf Club, and marked the occasion by giving his consent for the 'Royal' prefix to be used.

George V preferred hunting and shooting to golf, but his three sons all proved competent golfers having, no doubt, learnt the game on their grandfather's course at Windsor. In their turn they all became Captains of the Royal and Ancient Club: Edward VIII in 1922 (when Prince of Wales), George VI in 1930 (when Duke of York) and the Duke of Kent in 1937.

Edward VIII, who gave up the English throne to marry Mrs Simpson, made quite a success of the game. He twice achieved a hole in one, at Santos in Brazil and at Royal Wimbledon, and won a number of medal competitions at various golf clubs. He was captain of several clubs and played in the British Army Championship as a member of the Welsh Guards team. On his tours abroad a game of golf was always included in the itinerary. With the need for security less intense in those days, he was a spectator at several major professional tournaments, and once took part in a match in which the immortal American amateur, Bobby Jones, also played.

In 1924 George VI travelled to South Wales to play in an exhibition match as part of the opening ceremony for a nine-hole course in the Rhondda Valley, built by the local miners on their weekends off. In 1948 he visited Muirfield to see Henry Cotton win his third British Open Championship title. No members of the royal family in Britain take an active part in the game today, although royal patronage does still continue.

In other parts of Europe golf has been much favoured by royalty and several clubs bear the 'Royal' prefix. Belgium, in particular, boasts a number of monarchs who have excelled at golf. King Albert was enthusiastic, and inspired the founding of the Royal Golf Club de Belgique in 1906. King Leopold created a little piece of golfing history in 1939, when he played in the Belgian Amateur Championship at Le Zoute, the only reigning monarch ever to have played in a national championship. In 1949 he played in the French Amateur Championship at St Cloud and reached the quarter-finals.

King Baudouin, Leopold's son, inherited his father's talent for the game, to such an extent that he represented his country in the Belgium-France-Holland international match in 1958. The following year, entered as Mr B de Rethy, he partnered the Welsh professional Dai Rees in the Gleneagles Hotel pro-am tournament. King

Robert Sandow, former director of golf to the Shah of Iran, playing in the Douglas Bader Foundation tournament. 'Has anyone seen my ball?'

Constantine of Greece has also played in many pro-am events since being in exile. Prince Claus of the Netherlands, partnered by Peter Oosterhuis, the English professional now living in the United States, achieved a notable royal success when he won the pro-am which preceded the 1974 Dutch Open.

The most enthusiastic of the present monarchs is, without question, King Hassan of Morocco, who likes nothing better than playing golf in the company of well-known professionals In a recent major professional tournament in his country, he put up an additional prize for the winner of the event – a jewelled dagger reputed to be worth £30,000 (c $45,000).

In the 1970s the Shah of Iran set in motion an extensive programme for the construction of golf complexes in Iran, when he commissioned Robert Sandow, a former English professional golfer who turned to golf architecture after gaining a BSc in both agronomy and horticulture during the 1950s, to create a championship-style course on exotic Kish Island in the Persian Gulf. The project completed, the Shah appointed Mr Sandow as his director of golf responsible for the construction of further golf projects on the mainland. Alas, the ambitions of the Shah of Iran were thwarted by the revolution, and the Kish Island course now lies overgrown and unused.

On his return to Britain, Robert Sandow designed another course on land with royal connections: the majestic Rolls of Monmouth course in South Wales, so-called because it is situated in the Home Park of the Hendre Estate, which was once the home of Charles Stewart Rolls of Rolls-Royce fame. Indeed the building which now houses the clubhouse is the actual workshop where the famous Rolls-Royce engine was developed. Fringing the arboretum and bordering the third and fourth fairways can be seen two splendid sycamores. These trees were planted in 1900 by the Duke and Duchess of York, the future King George V and Queen Mary, during a seven-day visit to The Hendre, when they were driven from London by none other than C S Rolls. The room in which the royal pair stayed during their visit was in the west wing of the magnificent Jacobean-style mansion; it now looks out over the 18th green and is called the King's Room. The two holes which are graced by the royal sycamores are named, appropriately, the Duke of York and the Duchess of York.

PRIME MINISTERS AND PRESIDENTS

Arthur James Balfour, a Scot, was the first British prime minister to be addicted to golf, and it was enthusiasm for the game which prompted many of his fellow politicians to take up the sport in and around London during the latter part of the 19th century. The word soon spread that golf was an excellent way to relax at the end of a tiring day spent in the Houses of Parliament. Two other British prime ministers, David Lloyd George and Winston Churchill, often refreshed their minds by chasing after a golf ball. Douglas Caird, a leading writer on women's golf, has many fond memories of golf in the company of David Lloyd George, and he told me the delightful story of how, as a youngster, he caddied for his father, Sir Andrew Caird, then managing director of the *Daily Mail*, in a match against the famous British prime minister. Before starting the match Douglas was warned by his father that, being fed up with losing to the prime minister, should he lose again he would deduct sixpence from the customary fee he paid Douglas for his services as a caddy. Lose he did. Come lunchtime young Caird had to do without his favourite topping of fresh cream on his apple pie dessert because of lack of funds. On being told the reason why Douglas went without his

ABOVE LEFT Vice President Richard Nixon sinking a putt while President Eisenhower looks on, 1953.

LEFT President J F Kennedy enjoying a round of golf, 1963.

ABOVE President Ford and comedian Bob Hope relaxing as they wait to play at Eldorado Country Club, Palm Springs, 1975.

cream, the prime minister guffawed loudly before whispering to the waitress to serve the young man with a double helping. Douglas remembers clearly the prime minister ribbing his father and calling him the meanest Scottish journalist he had ever set eyes on. Returning to Sunningdale alone for lunch a little later in the week, Douglas was amazed to discover that the prime minister had left instructions with the head waiter to allow Douglas to order a double helping of fresh cream whenever he wished – compliments of the prime minister!

With the exception of Arnold Palmer, President Dwight D Eisenhower probably did more to boost the game of golf in the United States in the years immediately following the conclusion of World War II than any other person. Having returned from the war a conquering hero, he swept into the White House in 1953, and immediately arranged for a practice green and bunker to be constructed on the White House lawn. Whenever the opportunity arose to slip away from the pressures of government, he often headed for Augusta National Golf Club to indulge in his favourite sport. Eisenhower's arrival on the political scene coincided with the rise of television, and viewers were constantly being shown shots of their President chipping and putting either at Camp David or on the White House lawn, and sometimes playing with friends at Augusta. The cry of 'I Like Ike' rapidly changed to 'Like Ike I Wanna Play Golf'.

Then Arnold Palmer entered the scene and won everything in sight with his swashbuckling style of golf. He and the President soon became friends and now America had two national heroes. Golf became the 'in' game and millions of Americans quickly got into the swing of the new national pastime.

Gerald Ford also turned to golf for relaxation during his term of office. In 1975 he took part in the pro-am that preceded the Jackie Gleason Classic tournament. After his defeat in the election he played in the Memphis Classic pro-am and achieved a hole in one. In 1977 he introduced his own invitational tournament, and in 1978 the US PGA made him their first honorary member. He visited Britain three times in succession from 1981 onward to play in the Bob Hope Classic charity tournament. Ronald Reagan has long been a keen golfer and is often shown on television playing a shot or two.

The Royal and Ancient game of golf is indeed a game for all people.

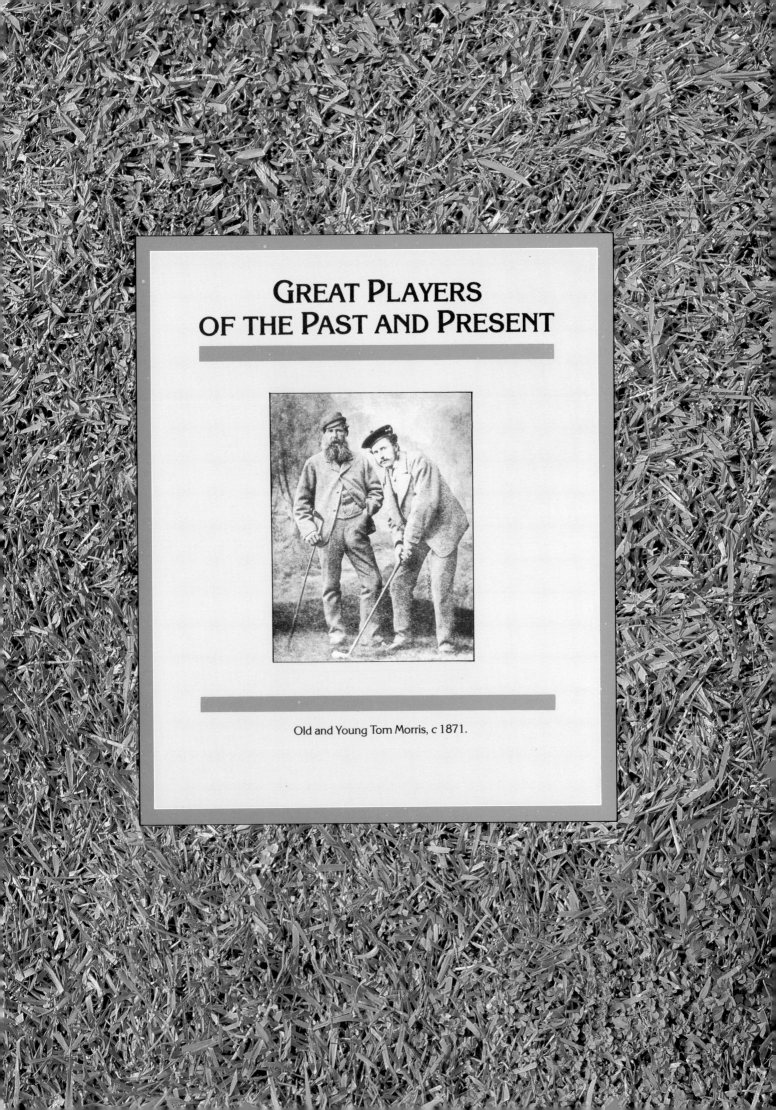

GREAT PLAYERS
OF THE PAST AND PRESENT

Old and Young Tom Morris, c 1871.

Someone once said (I believe it was Walter Hagen, but then again it could have been Ben Hogan): 'Anyone can win one major championship, but it takes a great player to win more than one.' He simply meant that one big win could be a fluke result.

In the annals of golf are the names of many golfers who found fame by winning a single major championship, and there are many more who became famous because of their failure to win when they should have. They were, of course, all endowed with a high degree of skill, otherwise they would not have been competing in such events in the first place, but one could write a book about gifted golfers who failed to achieve greatness.

This, however, is a chapter devoted to the great players – great not only because of the nerve and skill that enabled them to accumulate an impressive number of major achievements, but also for the way they modestly wore the mantle of success, thus creating the high standards and rich traditions that golfers everywhere still take care to maintain.

Allan Robertson, the first of the great players, won no major titles for he had the misfortune to be born in 1815 – 45 years before the British Open, the first of the four great championships, came into being. A product of the feather-ball age, he was known as 'Robertson the Unbeatable', because no one was able to match his re-markable skill in manoeuvring the unpredictable feathery round the windswept Scottish links. Even when he finally turned to using the gutta-percha ball, the ball he at first flatly refused to make or play with, he continued his unbeaten run in challenge matches. It has been said that he safeguarded his record by avoiding his two most dangerous challengers, Old Tom Morris ('Old' Tom to distinguish him from his brilliant son, 'Young' Tom) and Willie Park. But would Robertson's contemporary professionals have given him such an exalted title had he refused to play these two outstanding players? I think not.

Old Tom, like everyone else, held Robertson in high esteem, and described him as the most cunning player with club, cleek or putter he had ever played against. Indeed, had not an attack of jaundice ended his life in 1859, the year before the inaugural British Open Championship, Robertson's name might well have appeared among the early winners of the most coveted title in golf. A year prior to his death he astonished everyone by playing the Old Course at St Andrews in 79 strokes, the first time anyone had been under 80 there. After his death a member of St Andrews paid him a fitting tribute by saying: 'They may shut up their shops and toll their bells, for the greatest among them is gone.'

● TOM MORRIS, YOUNG ●
AND OLD

Old Tom Morris, besides being employed by Robertson as a ballmaker, often partnered the great man in foursome challenge matches and together they proved formidable opponents to anyone daring to throw out a challenge. The legendary match of the time was truly a marathon. It took place in 1849 between Robertson and Morris from St Andrews and the twin brothers, Willie and Jamie Dunn of Musselburgh. Played over three courses, Musselburgh, St Andrews and North Berwick, the St Andrews pair fought back brilliantly at North Berwick to win the match by two holes after being four holes down with only eight left to play.

Old Tom went on to learn his lessons well from Allan Robertson and quickly became a great player in his own right. In the early 1850s he left St Andrews to take up the job of professional at the newly opened Prestwick club, on the west coast of Scotland. It was there, in 1860,

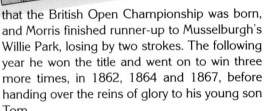

ABOVE LEFT Allan Robertson, 'The Unbeatable'.

ABOVE *On Musselburgh Links,* Charles Lees, c 1859.

LEFT Old Tom Morris (second from right), early in his career.

TOP RIGHT The Dyke hole at North Berwick, by John Smart, c 1889.

that the British Open Championship was born, and Morris finished runner-up to Musselburgh's Willie Park, losing by two strokes. The following year he won the title and went on to win three more times, in 1862, 1864 and 1867, before handing over the reins of glory to his young son Tom.

Young Tom Morris was without a doubt the greatest golfer of his generation. In a brief but brilliant career he won the Open Championship four times in a row to create a record which remains unequalled to this day. He also remains the youngest man to have won the Open, being only 17 years and five months old when he gained the first of his four titles in 1868. Having completed three wins in a row he was allowed to keep the championship belt as his own property and, with no trophy to contest, the Open Championship was not played in 1871. When it was revived the following year with a brand new trophy, Young Tom, continuing to dominate, won it again. To discover how highly talented Young Tom really was, one has only to look at his winning score of 149 at Prestwick in 1870. Scored over three rounds of the then 12-hole Prestwick course, this was remarkable scoring for the gutty-ball age, and his final round score of 47, which was one shot below level fours and included an eagle three at the 500 yards (445 m) first hole, was an incredible performance. In the remaining 32 years that the gutty ball was used, not one of the great players who followed Young Tom ever equalled his brilliant winning score. Sadly, in 1875, his illustrious career came to a tragic end a few months after he received the news that his wife had died in childbirth together with his newborn son. Devoted to his young wife, to whom he had been married for only one year, he failed to recover from the shock, and on Christmas Day he died of a 'broken heart' at the

ABOVE Willie Park senior – four-times winner of the Open Championship, in 1860, 1863, 1866 and 1875.

TOP RIGHT Willie Park junior, 1889.

ABOVE RIGHT Jamie Anderson, Open Champion in 1877, 1878 and 1879, was the second of four men to win the Championship three times in a row.

age of 24. The inscription on his tombstone in St Andrews Cathedral reads: 'Deeply regretted by numerous friends and all golfers, he thrice in succession won the championship belt and held it without rivalry and yet without envy, his many amiable qualities being no less acknowledged than his golfing achievements'.

Between them the Morrises had dominated the Championship by winning eight times in 12 years – a father and son record that it is safe to say will never be broken. Willie Park won the Championship four times and his son Willie junior won twice to come closest to matching the Morrises, but there it ends.

Straying from the great champions for a while, there was among them at that time a talented amateur golfer, Gilbert Mitchell-Innes, who, it is said, could play on level terms with these great players and occasionally beat them. It was he, so Bernard Darwin, the doyen of golf writers, tells us in his book *British Golf*, who was the author of the saying that the way to beat a professional is never to let him get a hole up. It would appear that, had Mitchell-Innes not pursued other interests and pastimes but concentrated on golf, his name might well have been added to the Open Championship winners' list. Young Tom Morris once remarked of him: 'I cannot understand Mr Innes when he's playing as fine a game as any mortal man ever played, leaving golf to run after stinking beasts and then coming back, not able to hit a ball at all.' He once partnered Young Tom in a 600-hole match against Jamie Anderson and Davie Strath, two outstanding professionals,

BOB FERGUSON

Bob Ferguson came within a whisker of equalling Young Tom Morris' record of four consecutive titles when, having tied with Willie Fernie of Dumfries in the Championship at Musselburgh in 1883, he lost the play-off after going to the last hole leading by one stroke.

LEFT A Spy cartoon of John Ball. Britain's greatest amateur, he won eight amateur championships and also the 1890 Open.

and he and his partner won by eight holes. When he did give the game some serious thought he twice won the St Andrews Silver Medal, in 1864 and 1874, and the St Andrews Royal Medal, in 1870.

His grandson, Norman Mitchell-Innes, still plays with a wooden putter that Gilbert often used when playing with the Morrises.

After Young Tom Morris we go on a few years before coming to two more golfers who achieved greatness through their exploits in the Open Championship. Each of these men won three titles in a row – Jamie Anderson of St Andrews in 1877, 1878 and 1879, and Bob Ferguson of Musselburgh in the following three years.

With two Championships under his belt, Willie Park junior all but made it three when he needed a short putt to tie with Harry Vardon at Prestwick in 1898, but he missed the putt and faded away from the Championship scene. He went on to make his mark in other branches of the game and found equal success in a clubmaking business and in golf-course architecture, Sunningdale Old Course, England, being one of his famous courses.

Going back to the early 1890s we must give a mention to John Ball and Harold Hilton, the two outstanding amateurs of the time and the first Englishmen to win the Open Championship. Ball, a member of the Royal Liverpool Club, won in 1890 at Prestwick, and achieved a notable double that year by also winning the British Amateur Championship at Hoylake. Between 1888 and 1912 he won the British Amateur title a record eight times. Hilton, also from the Royal Liverpool Club, won the Open in 1892 and repeated the feat in 1897. He was equally successful in major amateur championships, winning the British Amateur in 1900, 1901 and 1911, and the United States Amateur Championship in 1911. He was the author of several books on golf and the editor of *Golf Illustrated*.

Another famous amateur of this period who did much for golf with his writings on the game was Horace Hutchinson. He twice won the British Amateur, in 1886 and 1887, and in 1890 he finished in fifth place in the Open Championship. In 1908 he was elected captain of the Royal and Ancient Club, the first Englishman to receive the honour. Playing much of his golf at the Royal North Devon Club at Westward Ho! he is credited as the man who influenced John Henry Taylor to take up the game.

ABOVE LEFT Harold Hilton, the only British amateur to win the Open twice (1892 and 1897).

LEFT Horace Hutchinson by Spy.

ABOVE The Great Triumvirate – Taylor, Braid and Vardon – by Clement Flower, 1913.

● THE GREAT TRIUMVIRATE ●

John Henry Taylor, who often acted as Hutchinson's caddie at Westward Ho!, was the first English professional to win the British Open and, appropriately, he won it at Royal St Georges, Sandwich, in 1894, the first time the Championship moved out of Scotland and onto English soil. Taylor's name will forever be linked with those of Harry Vardon and James Braid. In a span of 21 years, beginning in 1894 and ending with World War I in 1914, they completely do-minated the British golfing scene by winning the Open Championship 16 times. It is no wonder they were dubbed the Great Triumvirate. In those 21 years Taylor won the Open five times, was runner-up three times and on two other occasions was joint runner-up. If that was not enough he added the British Professional Matchplay title to the list in 1904, won the French Open twice in succession in 1908 and 1909 and the German Open in 1912. In 1900 he

HARRY VARDON

Harry Vardon won the Open for the first time in 1896 and was 44 years old when he picked up his last title in 1914, a few months before the outbreak of World War I. Three times in succession from 1900 he had to be content with second place, and was again runner-up in 1912.

ABOVE RIGHT J H Taylor, c1912.

ABOVE FAR RIGHT Francis Ouimet, the young American amateur, broke the British-born domination of the US Open in 1913.

BELOW RIGHT Harry Vardon (white boots, back to camera) and J H Taylor (touching cap) during the play-off for the 1896 Open Championship at Muirfield.

was runner-up in the United States Open to his great friend and rival Harry Vardon.

Known to his friends as 'J H', Taylor was a dignified man and a credit to the game. In 1933 he was elected non-playing captain of the British Ryder Cup team and led his team to a rare victory over the Americans at Southport and Ainsdale. In 1950, at the age of 79, he was made an honorary member of the Royal and Ancient Golf Club, and on his 90th birthday the captain and past captains of the club again honoured him by presenting him with a silver salver suitably inscribed and bearing their signatures.

In 1957 Taylor was elected President of the Royal North Devon Golf Club – the club where he once eked out a living as a caddie had paid him the highest honour they could. His book *Golf, My Life's Work*, has now become a collectors' item. In 1963, at the grand old age of 92, he died where he had been born in the village of Northam overlooking the links of Westward Ho!

The second and most celebrated member of the Great Triumvirate was Harry Vardon. Every golfer in the world who has consulted a teaching manual will be familiar with his name on account of the 'Vardon grip', which is now the standard grip of the majority who play golf. His record of six victories in the British Open still stands, but the American, Tom Watson, with his five victories, is still young and capable enough to equal if not break the record during the next few years.

In January 1900 Vardon was persuaded to spend a year touring the United States, the object of the exercise being to promote a new ball called the Vardon Flyer. The ball, made of gutta-percha, was to have a limited life because it coincided with the advent of the Haskell rubber-cored ball.

For the game itself the tour proved to be an enormous success, as thousands flocked to watch the English genius in action in the many exhibition matches he played. While there he won the United States Open Championship, beating J H Taylor by two strokes. Vardon returned to America 13 years later hoping to repeat his victory, but he reckoned without the young American amateur, Francis Ouimet. Such was the British-born domination of the US Open at the time that everyone expected the winner to be either Ted Ray, the current British Open Champion, or Harry Vardon. The American, who decided to play in the event only because it took place in his home town, shocked the whole

of the golfing world by winning it after a play-off with the two great Englishmen.

Vardon returned to the United States in 1920 and to his credit finished joint runner-up in the US Open at the age of 50. Although he won only the one championship in the United States, his flowing style and accurate iron play left a lasting impression on young Americans, and it was he more than any other golfer of his time who gave American golf its initial boost. What is not generally known is that Vardon had a younger brother, Tom, who was also a top-class golfer, so much so that he finished second in the 1903 British Open behind his famous brother, was fourth in 1904, one stroke ahead of his brother, and joint third in 1907.

The last but not least of the Great Triumvirate was James Braid, a Scotsman who made golfing history by becoming the first man to win the British Open five times. Equally impressive as a matchplayer, in nine years he won four British Matchplay Championships. Legend has it that he owes his victories to finding two clubs, a driver and an aluminium-headed putter, that suited him. Before discovering these precious implements he struggled with length from the tee, and his putting was once described as so bad it was enough to make angels weep! Certainly something suddenly worked for him, for from the time he turned professional in 1893 he was to win nothing of note until 1901, when he made the breakthrough and won the first of his five British Open Championships, and with it the added satisfaction of leaving Vardon and Taylor trailing in his wake in second and third places, respectively. Braid had finally arrived, and thus was formed the famous trio who did more to popularize golf before World War I than any other players. In 1950 James Braid was elected honorary member of the Royal and Ancient Club, and in the same year he died in his London home at the age of 80.

Before leaving the period prior to World War I, a mention must be made of Willie Anderson, a talented Scottish professional who emigrated to the United States in 1895. The first man to win the US Open Championship four times (three of them in a row from 1903 to 1905), he also finished runner-up in 1897, was third once, fourth twice and fifth three times – a tremendous record that has never been equalled. Who knows what he might have achieved had he not died suddenly of arteriosclerosis at the early age of 32.

● THE FLAMBOYANT WALTER HAGEN ●

While the British were preparing for war there emerged in the United States a character, in every sense of the word, who was to take golf by the scruff of the neck and give it a thorough shaking. Indeed, Walter Hagen did more to take the starchiness out of the game – both on and off the course – than any other man. Not for him the swing-restricting tweed jackets and breeches; when he was on the course there was no mistaking him for anyone else. Colourful casual clothing and black and white shoes were his trademark. His play and his manner were as flamboyant as his dress. Here was the first of the truly

swashbuckling golfers who had the rare ability of scoring well from deep rough and other almost unplayable positions. Be it matchplay or strokeplay, golf to him was all about winning, and win he did in no uncertain fashion.

Making his breakthrough with victory in the United States Open in 1914, Hagen sat on his laurels for five years before suddenly bursting into action like a firecracker. In 1919 he again won the US Open, was US PGA Champion (it was then matchplay) in 1921, 1924, 1925, 1926 and 1927 and British Open Champion in 1922, 1924, 1928 and 1929.

ABOVE LEFT James Braid at the height of his career.

ABOVE Willie Anderson was the first man to win the US Open four times, in 1901, 1903, 1904 and 1905.

ABOVE RIGHT New York gives Bobby Jones a hero's welcome following his victory in the 1926 British Open.

When Hagen made his first trip to Britain to compete in the British Open, at Deal in 1920, he was politely informed that professionals were not allowed entry into the clubhouse. In typical Hagen fashion he hired a Rolls-Royce and a suitably dressed butler, and parked outside the main windows of the clubhouse where he lunched on smoked salmon, caviar, champagne and all the trimmings. The club members had the last laugh on this occasion because Hagen could do no better than finish in last but one place in the Championship.

Hagen quickly came to terms with the British seaside courses, and emerged triumphant in 1922 at Royal St George's Sandwich to become the first American-born player to win the British Open. Unimpressed by the prize money he received at the presentation ceremony, he promptly handed the cheque to his caddie. At Troon the following year, when he finished runner-up to Arthur Havers, Hagen took another embarrassing dig at those who looked upon professionals as second-class citizens. Being told that a concession by the committee allowed the presentation to be made inside the clubhouse and that he had been invited to attend, Hagen declined the offer, turned to the crowd and invited them to join him at a party he was throwing at a local inn. In a single sentence the golf writer Bernard Darwin described perfectly the greatness of Walter Hagen: 'The difference between Hagen and other players is that he just wins and they just don't'.

THE GREATEST OF ALL AMATEURS

The arrival of Walter Hagen marked the almost complete domination of major championship golf by American players, which was to last for no less than 20 years. Playing a major part in the American dominance was one Robert Tyre Jones Junior, from Atlanta, Georgia, an amateur who, with the exception of Jack Nicklaus, is the greatest golfer ever to set foot on a golf course. In a short but brilliant career he became the idol of the ordinary club golfer. For here was a man who, like themselves, played the game purely for the glory of winning once in a while without any thought of gaining rich rewards — a true-blue amateur in every sense of the word.

In a space of eight years from 1923 to 1930 Jones amassed an incredible total of 13 major titles. A measure of his amazing ability is the fact that he played hardly any competitive golf outside the 'big ones', much preferring to play friendly matches with his friends. He practised little, and often entered the championships with only a warm-up beforehand. In 1930 he achieved the ultimate when he won what was then regarded as the Grand Slam of golf — the Open and Amateur titles of both Britain and the United States — a feat that will probably remain unequalled.

With these four historic victories under his belt in the space of a single year Jones, feeling there was nothing worthwhile left to achieve, decided enough was enough and announced his retirement from top-class competitive golf at the tender age of 28. His outstanding achievements were recognized by the United States and Great Britain in several ways. After winning his first British Open at Royal Lytham in 1926 he arrived home to a tumultuous ticker-tape welcome in New York City. His picture also appeared on a national postage stamp, one of the few golfers to receive this honour. In 1958 he made a nostalgic return to Scotland to receive the freedom of the Burgh of St Andrews. When he had first played on the Old Course at St Andrews in 1921 he had hated it so much that he tore his card up in frustration halfway through his fourth round of the British Open. But as the years rolled by he grew to love the place and afterward declared it his favourite golf course.

During World War II Jones served with the US Army, rising to the rank of lieutenant-colonel,

WALTER HAGEN

Walter Hagen was a Ryder Cup player and captain in all five matches between 1927 and 1935 and non-playing captain in 1937, when he led the American team to a first-ever Ryder Cup victory on British soil.

GENE SARAZEN

Gene Sarazen is another great golfer from the Hagen and Jones era who dented the pride of the British golfer. Born Eugene Saraceni in Harrison, New York, the son of Italian immigrants, he changed his name because it sounded more suited to a violinist than a golfer.

RIGHT Henry Cotton became Open Champion for the third time at Muirfield in 1948.

ABOVE RIGHT Sweet-swinging Sam Snead, 1962.

BELOW FAR RIGHT A rare shot of Ben Hogan hitting out of deep rough, 1938.

but on returning home he began to suffer from a muscular disease called syringomyelia which eventually confined him to a wheelchair. He finally gave up a long and brave battle against the disease in 1971 and died in Atlanta, Georgia, at the age of 69. It was a sad end for a great champion and a great man whose record reads: US Open Champion 1923, 1926, 1929 and 1930; British Open Champion 1926, 1927 and 1930; US Amateur Champion 1924, 1925, 1927, 1928 and 1930; British Amateur Champion 1930; Walker Cup appearances 1922, 1924, 1926, 1928 and 1930. His name is immortalized not only in the record books but also in one of the world's greatest golf courses at Augusta, which he created along with what is one of the major championships of modern times, the United States Masters, staged there every April.

Gene Sarazen made his niche in golfing history by becoming the first man to win the world's four major championships – the British Open, US Open, US PGA Championship and the

United States Masters. Only three others, Ben Hogan, Jack Nicklaus and Gary Player, have equalled the feat. At the age of 71 he accepted an invitation to play at Troon, in the 1973 British Open. By coincidence, it marked the 50th anniversary of his undistinguished debut in the British Open, on the very same course, when he failed to qualify. However, this time he created a sensation when, partnered by two other past champions, Max Faulkner and Fred Daly, and in full view of the television cameras, he holed in one at Troon's famous Postage Stamp eighth hole. As recently as April 1987 millions of television viewers saw Gene Sarazen teeing off with two other American greats of the past, Sam Snead and Byron Nelson, when they started off the American Masters at Augusta National, Florida. Not bad for an 85-year-old senior citizen.

● HENRY COTTON'S ● FAMOUS ROUND

The almost complete stranglehold that American golfers had on the British Open for 13 years was finally broken by Henry Cotton, a former London public schoolboy who made up his mind while still at school to become a professional golfer and a champion in the bargain. Such was his burning desire to succeed that he weekly hit thousands of balls in practice and in his own words: 'Chipped and putted for such a time it was easier to stay bent than to stand up'. His dedication was rewarded when he won the Open by five strokes at Royal St George's, Sandwich, in 1934. The 65 which he scored in the second round was then the lowest round ever recorded in the British Open, and led to the famous Dunlop '65' ball being made to commemorate the occasion. He won again in 1937 at Carnoustie, a win that gave him much satisfaction, for he took on and beat the mighty Americans who were there in force as part of the visiting Ryder Cup team. Had not World War II put an end to the Championship for six years who knows what records he might have created? He was then in his prime and the most talented player in Europe.

As it was, Cotton still managed one more Open victory after the war. This came at Muirfield in 1948 when, aged 41, he broke the course record by scoring 66 in the second round. He had been invalided out of the RAF when the war ended, and he did much work to help raise funds for the Red Cross. In recognition of this he was made an MBE. Like Walter Hagen before him, he also did much to further the cause of his fellow professionals. After receiving his cheque for winning the French Open in 1946, he let it be known quite clearly that it was an insult to his profession. His maxim was that if sponsors wanted the best players in the world, they should expect to pay them well.

As well as being three-times winner of the British Open, Cotton won the British Matchplay Championship three times and numerous other national championships on the Continent. He played in the Ryder Cup matches of 1929, 1937 and 1947 and was non-playing captain in 1953. For many years the Grand Old Man of British golf, Cotton sadly died on 23 December, 1987, at the age of 80, after suffering a short illness. A few days later he received a posthumous knight-

hood for his services to golf, the first golfer ever to receive such an honour.

Henry Cotton proved to be the last of the great British players, and only Tony Jacklin, when he won the British Open in 1969 and the US Open in 1970, has since caused a flutter in the hearts of the success-starved British golf fan. However, the demands put on the talented young Jacklin at the height of his success proved too much and he gradually faded out of the tournament scene. Nevertheless, he still remains very much in the limelight as the successful non-playing captain of the Great Britain and Europe Ryder Cup team.

● HOGAN COMES BACK ●
FROM INJURY

While Cotton was continuing his lone battle to put British golf back at the top, the United States was producing a new crop of great golfers in the

shapes of Ben Hogan, Sam Snead and Byron Nelson. All three were born in the same year (1912), and from 1937 to 1955 they amassed among them 21 major title wins. Without a doubt Hogan was the greatest player of the three, and is regarded by many as the supreme golfer of the modern era. His impressive record tells us that he won the US Open four times; the British Open once; the US PGA twice and the Masters twice. However, what it does not tell us is that in 1949 Hogan was involved in a horrendous car smash that almost ended his life. Multiple injuries, which included a broken leg, ankle, shoulder and pelvis, convinced everyone that Hogan's golf career was over. Hogan, however, had other ideas. As soon as he was declared fit enough to leave the hospital, he went home to Fort Worth, Texas, to practise in secret. By sheer determination, guts and a lot of gruelling effort, he made an amazing comeback and went on to win the 1950 US Open after a play-off with George Fazio and Lloyd Mangrum. Indeed,

six of the nine major championships he won came after his serious injuries. Despite being known as 'The Hawk' in the United States and 'The Iceman' in Britain, because of the way he shunned publicity and refused to give his autograph, the crowds loved him and flocked in the thousands to watch him play. He now lives in quiet retirement in Fort Worth.

Sam Snead first started to play 'golf' by cutting suitable branches from trees and shaping them into makeshift golf clubs to play on waste ground near his home in Hot Springs, Virginia. Progressing to 'real' golf, he learnt how to win the hard way by betting on himself to win without a dollar in his pocket to pay out should he ever have lost. It was in this tough school that he perfected the slow, sweet swing which earned him the nickname 'Swinging Sam'. It was this casual repeating action which helped him to carry on competing at the top well into his 60s. In 1974, at the age of 62, he amazingly finished in third place in the US PGA, three strokes

FAR LEFT Bing Crosby shares a joke with Byron Nelson.

BELOW FAR LEFT Bobby Locke, one of the finest putters the world of golf has ever known.

BELOW LEFT Peter Thomson remains the greatest golfer to come out of Australia, 1962.

ABOVE Arnold Palmer, the first golfing media star.

and Snead, could well have added more championships to this impressive list. He played in two Ryder Cup matches, in 1937 and 1947, and was non-playing captain in 1965. Retiring from competitive golf in the early 1950s, Nelson found success both as a teacher and television commentator on the game. In 1974 he was awarded the Bobby Jones Award in recognition of his outstanding contribution to golf.

● BOBBY LOCKE AND ●
PETER THOMSON

While the American stars concentrated mainly on their own circuit during this era, it was left to two other great overseas players, South African Bobby Locke and Peter Thomson of Australia, to dominate the British Open. Locke had already proved he was as good as the Americans by winning seven tournaments in the United States in the summer of 1947. Had he not become disillusioned with the American tournament scene, brought about as a result of his being refused the same appearance money offered to Americans, he probably would have won a number of major championships there. Turning his back on American golf he concentrated all his efforts on the British Open, which he won four times between 1949 and 1957. A slow, meticulous player, especially on the greens, he took great care over every shot. One of the greatest putters in the world, he won the Open Championships of many countries in all parts of the world, and won the South African Open Championship nine times between 1935 and 1955. A great player and a gentleman, he died in 1987 at the age of 69.

Many fine golfers have come from Australia, but Peter Thomson is still regarded as the greatest Australian golfer of them all. His early victories in the British Open are looked upon by some as not counting for much because they were achieved at a time when the American players were not appearing regularly. Nevertheless, he is the only man this century to achieve a hat-trick of victories in the Open Championship (1954, 1955 and 1956). The following year he came close to making it four in a row when he finished runner-up to Bobby Locke. In 1958 he won again to make it four wins and two seconds in the space of six years (he came second to Ben Hogan in 1953). In 1965 at Royal Birkdale he silenced his critics by winning again, this time

behind the winner, Lee Trevino. Three times the winner of both the Masters and the US PGA, he also won the British Open at his second attempt, in 1946. Fate decreed that he should never win the US Open, but he came close four times, finishing runner-up on each occasion. With a tournament career of almost 200 victories, he now plays for fun with a swing that looks as good as ever.

Byron Nelson achieved his first major breakthrough in 1937 with a victory in the Masters, a win he repeated again in 1942. He also won the US PGA title twice, in 1940 and 1945, and the US Open in 1939. In 1945 he recorded an incredible sequence of tournament victories, winning 11 in a row. But for the war he, like Hogan

ABOVE Jack Nicklaus and Arnold Palmer recall old memories during the 1987 US Masters.

with all the top Americans in the field including Tony Lema, the holder, Arnold Palmer and Jack Nicklaus. With this win he joined J H Taylor and James Braid as a five-time winner of the Championship. A quiet, likeable person, Peter Thomson is now enjoying much success playing on the American Seniors' tour.

● PALMER MAKES A MILLION ●

Arnold Palmer may not have been the greatest golfer in the world, but he was certainly the most exciting. When he played golf he was Tarzan, Errol Flynn and Superman rolled into one. To him there was just one way to hit a golf ball – an almighty swipe in the right general direction. If it landed in jungle it mattered little; a quick swashbuckling, superhuman stroke would get it flying back on course. He played a type of game (only better) that thousands played every weekend, and they loved him for it. Coming on the scene when television was in its infancy, he was the television producers' dream. Here was the guy-next-door making good, and it made for good viewing. He loved going for broke from impossible positions. In 1960, when all seemed lost, he won both the Masters and the US Open with last-round charges.

The British took him to their hearts when he went to St Andrews to play in the centenary Open of 1960. He lost by one stroke to the Australian Kel Nagle, but the fact that he was there triggered off a revival of American interest in the great event. The following year he was back and won at Royal Birkdale, and in 1962, at Troon, he successfully defended the title. He captured the imagination of people of all ages and thousands took up the game. As box-office material he rivalled the film stars. His picture appeared everywhere, on magazine covers, billboard hoardings and television commercials – Arnie had arrived, and he quickly became a multi-millionaire. The way he played was not a gimmick, it was the only way he knew how to play the game – hit it hard and get it into the hole as quickly as possible.

Behind the aggression on the course Arnold Palmer has a quiet, gentle nature, completely unaffected by his successful rise to stardom. No one really cared if he won or not so long as he entertained them with his swashbuckling style, but for the record he was: British Open Champion 1961 and 1962; US Open Champion 1960; Masters Champion 1958, 1960, 1962 and 1964; US Amateur Champion 1954; Ryder Cup player 1961, 1963, 1965, 1967, 1971 and 1973, and non-playing captain 1975.

● THE MAN IN BLACK ●

When Gary Player left his home in South Africa to try his luck as a professional golfer in Great Britain in 1955, no one dreamt that here was a man who was destined to become one of the all-time greats of golf. Small in stature at 5ft 7ins (1.70 m) and 154 lb (69.85 kg), he looked not to possess the physique and stamina required of a champion. But to his everlasting credit he set out to prove that fitness and strength allied to talent were more important than size. His dedication to fitness and practice bordered on the fanatical. Every spare minute was taken up with exercise – running, jumping, skipping, press-ups, weight training and practising golf shots. It was Player who invented the saying: 'The more I practise, the luckier I become'. He lived on a special diet and even took to wearing black clothing because he was told that black attracted the sun's rays, which would give him extra strength. He also trained his mind to be positive at all times. Fanatical it may have seemed, but the belief that what he was doing was the way to success certainly paid off handsomely for the diminutive South African.

Player gained his first big success in 1959 with victory in the British Open at Muirfield, a feat he repeated in 1968 and 1974, thus producing a remarkable treble of Open victories spanning three decades. In 1961 he became the first non-American to win the Masters, and also topped the money-winners' list for that year. In 1965 he became the first South African to win the US Open and with that win the first non-American to win the world's four major championships. Altogether he totalled nine major titles, the last being the Masters in 1978. He won the British Open three times, the Masters three times, the US PGA twice and the US Open once. He also won the South African Open 13 times and the Australian Open seven times. Still as fit as ever, he made the last round

BELOW Gary Player, the great South African golfer, in full swing.

BELOW RIGHT The greatest of them all, Jack Nicklaus, playing in the 1987 US Open.

in the Masters tournament at Augusta in 1987. Not bad for a 52-year-old! It is no wonder he is ranked alongside Arnold Palmer and Jack Nicklaus as one of the 'Big Three'.

● THE GREATEST OF ALL ●

One only has to look at Jack Nicklaus' record in the major championships to realize he is the greatest golfer of all time. In the 25 years since he turned professional in 1962, he has won 18 of the world's premier championships. Add the two US Amateur titles he won in 1959 and 1961 to the total and it puts him seven ahead of Bobby Jones, who was his boyhood idol. In 1959, at the age of 19, Nicklaus became the youngest winner of the US Amateur Championship for 50 years. Also as an amateur, in 1960, he finished runner-up to Palmer in the US Open. He is the only man to win the four major titles three times, and in 1972 he came within two strokes of achieving the Grand Slam in the same year. The most successful golfer in the history of the game, he is still, at 47, trying to add to his impressive total of major titles. In 1986 he caused a sensation by winning the Masters for the sixth time – this 24 years after winning his first major tournament. In 1987 he rose to the Masters' challenge once more, but faded away in the last couple of holes.

JACK NICKLAUS

Jack Nicklaus' record, of winning the British Open three times, the US Open four times, the US PGA five times, the Masters six times and the US Amateur twice, will almost certainly never be beaten, and who knows, he may yet add a few more titles to the list before he decides to retire.

Like the other two members of the 'Big Three', Arnold Palmer and Gary Player, Jack Nicklaus is a credit to his profession both on and off the golf course.

Lee Trevino, a contemporary of Jack Nicklaus, first shot into the limelight when he finished fifth in the US Open at Baltusrol in 1967, having borrowed the money from his wife, Claudia, to enter the event. Born in Dallas, Texas, in 1939, he was the last person anyone would have predicted to become an ordinary golfer, let alone a professional and a champion. His background was such that he never knew his father, whom he was named after, and neither his Mexican mother nor his grandfather could read or write. He learnt to play golf after being offered a job at a local driving range, and like Sam Snead before him, he supplemented his earnings by becoming a hustler at the game.

In 1968 Lee Trevino surprised the golfing world by winning the US Open at Oak Hill, New York, scoring below 70 in every round – still the only man to achieve this feat. Proving that his victory was no fluke, he won the title again in 1971, beating the great Jack Nicklaus in a play-off at Merion, Ardmore. A few weeks later he joined a select band of players who have won the US Open and the British Open in the same year – Bobby Jones, Gene Sarazen and Ben Hogan being the others.

A man who loves to crack jokes and talk and laugh with the crowd in between shots, Trevino is truly the clown prince of the fairways. But inwardly he is a person of deep compassion and generosity. When he won the Hawaiian Open in 1968 he gave most of his money to the family of Ted Makalena, a colleague who was killed in a surfing accident. During the 1976 Western Open he almost lost his own life when struck by lightning. Despite surgery on his back, which forced him into semi-retirement, he bounced back in typical Trevino style to win the 1984 US PGA title and in doing so amazingly scored in the 60s in all four rounds to repeat what he had accomplished 15 years previously in the US Open.

The greatest exponent of the wedge shot the world has ever seen, Trevino has won the British Open, the US Open and the US PGA titles twice each, but sadly the Masters title has eluded him. In 1985, having seen action with six Ryder Cup teams, he was selected as non-playing captain of the American team, a fitting finale to a brilliant career.

LEFT Lee Trevino, the 'Clown Prince of Golf', is the finest exponent of the classic wedge shot.

ABOVE Tom Watson, US Open Champion in 1982, is looking to win the British Open one more time to equal Harry Vardon's record six wins.

Gene Sarazen

GENE SARAZEN
Born 1902

British Open Champion: 1932
US Open Champion: 1922,
1932
US PGA Champion: 1922,
1923, 1933
US Masters Champion: 1935

HENRY COTTON
1907–1987

British Open Champion: 1934,
1937, 1948

Henry Cotton

Ben Hogan

BEN HOGAN
Born 1912

British Open Champion: 1953
US Open Champion: 1948,
1950, 1951, 1953
US PGA Champion: 1946, 1948
US Masters Champion: 1951,
1953

SAM SNEAD
Born 1912

British Open Champion: 1946
US PGA Champion: 1942,
1949, 1951
US Masters Champion: 1949,
1952, 1954

BYRON NELSON
Born 1912

US Open Champion: 1939
US PGA Champion: 1940, 1945
US Masters Champion: 1937,
1942

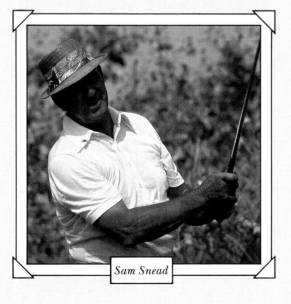

Sam Snead

Byron Nelson

Allan Robertson

ALLAN ROBERTSON
1815 - 1859

- - - - -

TOM MORRIS SENIOR
1821 - 1908

British Open Champion: 1861,
1862, 1864, 1867

- - - - -

TOM MORRIS JUNIOR
1851 - 1875

British Open Champion: 1868,
1869, 1870, 1872

- - - - -

J H TAYLOR
1871 - 1963

British Open Champion: 1894,
1895, 1900, 1909, 1913

Tom Morris Senior

Tom Morris
Junior

JAMES BRAID
1870 - 1950

British Open Champion: 1901,
1905, 1906, 1908, 1910

J H Taylor

HARRY VARDON
1870 - 1937

British Open Champion: 1896,
1898, 1899, 1903, 1911, 1914
US Open Champion: 1900

- - - - -

WALTER HAGEN
1892 - 1969

British Open Champion: 1922,
1924, 1928, 1929
US Open Champion: 1914,
1919
US PGA Champion: 1921,
1924, 1925, 1926, 1927

Harry
Vardon

James Braid

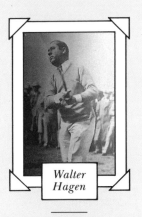

Walter
Hagen

BOBBY JONES
1902 - 1971

British Open Champion: 1926,
1927, 1930
US Open Champion: 1923,
1926, 1929, 1930

Bobby Jones

● WATSON'S GREAT ●
MATCHES

Tom Watson and Severiano Ballesteros, two players with contrasting styles, are the last of the established modern greats still with a realistic chance of adding to their tally of major championship titles. Watson, although picking up his first title when winning the British Open at Carnoustie in 1975, will long be remembered for his epic duel in the British sun with Jack Nicklaus at Turnberry in 1977. With both players tied after three days with identical rounds of 68–70–65, the last day produced the most exciting, nail-biting, heart-pounding, man-to-man last-round encounter in the history of the Championship. And what a climax – still tied with two holes remaining, Watson broke the deadlock by rolling in a putt from off the edge of the 17th green. When all seemed lost for Nicklaus at the final hole, he looked to have forced a play-off by sinking a monster putt for a birdie. Watson, now needing to hole his putt for a birdie and the title, did so and the crowd erupted. Watson had scored a 65 to Nicklaus' 66. (Happily, a video recording has since been produced of this historic match.)

Nicklaus suffered another dramatic defeat at the hands of Watson in the 1982 US Open at Pebble Beach, when the latter chipped in from an impossible position at the 17th hole to swing the result in his favour when Nicklaus looked the certain winner. With five wins to his name in the British Open, Watson now needs but one more to equal the six achieved by Harry Vardon. He almost did it at St Andrews in 1984, foiled only by Ballesteros, who won with a par-birdie finish which Watson could not match. Two Masters titles, in 1977 and 1981, bring Watson's total of major wins to eight, and although championship wins have eluded him during the last few years he is still young enough to make a comeback.

● THE SWASHBUCKLING ●
SPANIARD

Unlike the American Tom Watson, with his crisp, rhythmic swing, Severiano Ballesteros looks to have come out of the same mould that produced Arnold Palmer, especially when performing one of his famous last nine-hole charges. Ballesteros first served notice that he possessed

the exceptional talent to become a great player when, aged just 19, he entered the British Open at Royal Birkdale in 1976 and almost pulled off a sensational victory. He led for three rounds, only to fall at the last hurdle to give Johnny Miller the title. Nevertheless, finishing in a tie for second place with the great Jack Nicklaus, he had made his mark on the championship.

Born in Pedrena, Spain, in 1957, Ballesteros learnt to play by hitting stones with a makeshift golf club on the beaches near his humble home. He was drawn to the game because one of the best Spanish golfers of that time, Raymond Sota, was his mother's brother. Seve practised for countless hours on the lonely beaches, determined one day to emulate his favourite uncle. Before the start of the 1979 British Open at Royal Lytham, the experts were saying that the rough was so severe that the man who could consistently keep his ball on the fairways would be the eventual winner. Ballesteros proved them wrong by deliberately aiming for the rough from the tee rather than run the risk of putting his ball in the dangerous fairway bunkers. With amazing consistency in all four rounds he smashed his ball onto the greens from the deep rough. The effect on the rest of the field was one of de-moralization as the swashbuckling Spaniard swung his way to an incredible victory. He captured not only the coveted trophy but also the hearts of the public like no other since Arnold Palmer, and with his film-star looks he quickly became the most marketable golfer ever to come out of Europe – and continues to be so to this very day. Without a doubt he has done more for European golf than any other player, and to his credit he has not entirely abandoned the European tournament circuit.

In 1980 Ballesteros went to the United States and became the first European to win the Masters title, a performance he repeated in 1983. He all but did it again in 1987, losing in a three-man play-off which was won by the young American Larry Mize. Ballesteros' victory at St Andrews in 1984 gave him his second British Open title and his fourth major title in all. As a matchplayer he is the most difficult of men to beat, as he proved when helping the Great Britain and Europe Ryder Cup team to historic victories against the Americans at The Belfry in 1985 and at Muirfield Village, Ohio, in 1987. Still winning tournaments with amazing regularity all round the world, Ballesteros continues to be the most exciting European golfer ever seen.

LEFT Seve Ballesteros in full flow.

ABOVE A triumphant Seve winning the Masters for the second time in three years, 1983.

JACK NICKLAUS
Born 1940

British Open Champion: 1966,
1970, 1978
US Open Champion: 1962,
1967, 1972, 1980
US PGA Champion: 1963,
1971, 1973, 1975, 1980
US Masters Champion: 1963,
1965, 1966, 1972, 1975, 1986

———

LEE TREVINO
Born 1939

British Open Champion: 1971,
1972
US Open Champion: 1968,
1971
US PGA Champion: 1974, 1984

———

Jack Nicklaus

Lee Trevino

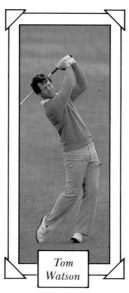

*Tom
Watson*

———

TOM WATSON
Born 1949

British Open Champion: 1975,
1977, 1980, 1982, 1983
US Open Champion: 1982
US Masters Champion: 1977,
1981

———

SEVERIANO BALLESTEROS
Born 1957

British Open Champion: 1979,
1984
US Masters Champion: 1980,
1983

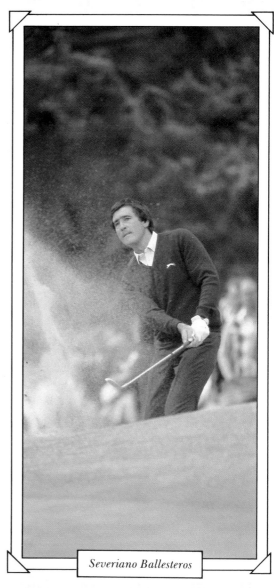

Severiano Ballesteros

Peter Thomson

BOBBY LOCKE
1918-1987

British Open Champion: 1949,
1950, 1952, 1957

PETER THOMSON
Born 1929

British Open Champion: 1954,
1955, 1956, 1958, 1965

Bobby Locke

ARNOLD PALMER
Born 1929

British Open Champion: 1961,
1962
US Open Champion: 1960
US Masters Champion: 1958,
1960, 1962, 1964

GARY PLAYER
Born 1935

British Open Champion: 1959,
1968, 1974
US Open Champion: 1965
US PGA Champion: 1962, 1972
US Masters Champion: 1961,
1974, 1978

Gary
Player

Arnold Palmer

● THE LADIES ●

The first really outstanding woman golfer in the world was Cecilia Leitch, who was born at Silloth, Cumberland, in 1891. Known by all as Cecil, she first came into prominence by reaching the semi-finals of the British Women's Championship in 1908 at the age of 17. In 1914 she won the title for the first time, and when the Championship was resumed a few years after World War I, she collected the title three more times – the last being in 1926.

Cecilia Leitch also won the French Ladies' Open five times between 1912 and 1924, the Canadian Ladies' Open in 1921 and was twice the English Women's champion, in 1914 and 1921 – an impressive array of victories.

ABOVE LEFT Glenna Collet, winner of six US Women's Amateur titles between 1922 and 1935.

ABOVE Kathy Whitworth – the first woman golfer to record career earnings of $1-million.

LEFT Cecil Leitch at the age of 19.

• JOYCE WETHERED •

Miss Leitch's greatest rival was Joyce Wethered (now Lady Heathcote Amory) who went on to become the greatest woman golfer of her time. As a 19-year-old unknown she caused a sensation by defeating Miss Leitch in the final of the English Women's Championship at Sheringham, Norfolk, in 1920. With that win under her belt, she remained unbeaten in the event for five successive years. Bobby Jones paid her the compliment of saying she was the finest golfer of either sex he had ever seen. Born in 1901 at Witley, Surrey, her greatest triumphs were in the British Women's Amateur Championship, which she won four times, in 1922, 1924, 1925 and 1929. She also won the French Ladies' Open in 1921. On her way to winning the British title in 1925 she prevailed over the United States champion, Glenna Collett, when they met in the third round. The next time she was to play Miss Collett was in the final at St Andrews in 1929 and again she emerged triumphant over the American, winning by 3 and 1 after being five holes down at one stage.

After this victory Miss Wethered went into semi-retirement, playing only in foursomes events. She won the Worplesdon Foursomes title eight times with seven different partners. In 1935 she was persuaded to turn professional and made a tour of America. There she played in exhibition matches with Bobby Jones, Gene Sarazen and Babe Zaharias. During her stay she played in 52 matches and earned many thousands of dollars.

• THE ALL-ROUND BABE •

Babe Zaharias ranks as the first of the great American women golfers. Born Mildred Didrikson at Port Arthur, Texas, in 1914, she became known as 'The Babe' after winning seven track and field events in the American Athletic Championships of 1931 when just a 17-year-old. A brilliant athlete, she won gold medals at the 1932 Olympics in the javelin and 80-metre hurdles before deciding to turn seriously to golf.

In 1954 Babe Zaharias surprised everyone by winning her third US Open title after having undergone major surgery for cancer the previous year. During her professional career Zaharias won 31 tournaments in all, seven of them after her operation. Having fought bravely against the disease she finally lost the struggle and died in 1956.

During the early 1930s there appeared on the scene an English girl named Pamela Barton who looked to be destined for a brilliant career in women's golf. She was only 17 when, in 1934, she won the French Ladies' Open. Two years later she caused a stir on both sides of the Atlantic by winning both the British and American Amateur titles within the space of a month. Typical of many of the young British women of that time, she volunteered to serve in the forces when Britain declared war on Germany, and left home to join the Women's Auxiliary Air Force. In the winter of 1943, aged only 26, she was tragically killed when the plane in which she was travelling crashed in Kent.

BABE ZAHARIAS

In 1946 Zaharias won the US Women's Amateur title and the following year the British Women's title. Having achieved this notable double she joined the professional ranks and found immediate success by winning the US Women's Open at Atlantic City in 1948 and again in 1950 at Rolling Hills.

LEFT Jo-Anne Carner, born in 1939, is still a force to be reckoned with on the US women's professional circuit.

ABOVE Catherine Lacoste, the French sensation.

ABOVE RIGHT Pam Barton looked destined for a brilliant career in golf, but was tragically killed in an air crash, in 1943, during war service with the RAF.

FAR RIGHT One of the United States' all-time golfing greats, Nancy Lopez.

Two Americans who did much for the professional circuit in the early days were Patty Berg and Louise Suggs. Before joining the professional ranks, where she won 41 tournaments, Patty Berg won the US Women's Amateur Championship in 1938. Helping to form the Ladies' Professional Golf Association with eleven others, she gained the distinction of becoming its first president.

Louise Suggs, the daughter of a golf professional, made her mark in amateur golf by winning both the British and US Amateur titles. In reward for her long list of achievements she was elected president of the LPGA in 1956-57.

● WRIGHT AND WHITWORTH ● RECORDS

Mickey Wright turned professional in 1954 and made a remarkable success of playing golf for a living. Her record 82 tournament wins included four US Opens and four LPGA titles. When she was born in 1935 in San Diego, California, she was named Mary Kathryn, but her attorney father, expecting a boy, had already chosen Michael as the name, and it is by this name she has become known. In 1961 she created a tournament record by winning 10 events – four of them in a row, including the US Open. Not surprisingly, she was leading money-winner several times during the height of her career. Ranked as one of the greatest women golfers of all time, she is a member of the LPGA Hall of Fame.

If Mickey Wright was successful, Kathy Whitworth was even more so. She entered the professional ranks as Miss Wright was ceasing to compete on a full-time basis. In a lucrative period between 1963 and 1973, she had 70 tournament victories to her name, and in 1982 she recorded her 83rd victory to beat the record of Mickey Wright. The previous year she had set up an amazing record by becoming the first woman golfer to reach total career earnings of $1-million – quite a feat for someone who won no money at all in her first six months and only picked up a mere $30 when she first got among the prizewinners. In 1975 she joined Mickey Wright as a member of the LPGA Hall of Fame.

When Jo-Anne Carner finally decided to join the professional tournament scene in 1969, when she was 30, she left behind her an impressive amateur career which included five US

Women's Amateur Championships. Born Jo-Anne Gunderson in Massachusetts in 1939, she first came into prominence in 1956 when, still at high school, she won the US Junior Girls' title. Her physique, powerful hitting and extrovert personality have resulted in her being affectionately nicknamed 'Big Momma' by her professional colleagues. In 1981 she topped $1-million in career earnings and is now fast approaching an all-time record of $2-million. She is still participating on the US professional circuit and her many victories include two US Open Championships. In 1982 she was elected to the LPGA Hall of Fame, having the previous year become only the fifth woman golfer to receive the Bobby Jones Award for her outstanding contribution to the game. Had she remained an amateur there is little doubt that she would have exceeded the total of six US Women's Amateur titles that Glenna Collett (later Mrs Edwin Vare), achieved between 1922 and 1935.

● THE PRECOCIOUS ●
FRENCHWOMAN

One who preferred to remain an amateur was the French sensation Catherine Lacoste, the daughter of Wimbledon tennis champion, René Lacoste, and Simone de la Chaume, a British Women's Amateur Champion. Miss Lacoste, having won everything of note in France, decided it was time to take on the professionals at their own game and crossed the Atlantic to compete in the US Open. The year was 1967 and the field included the top American professionals of the day. Ignored by the media and competitors alike, she created the biggest sensation the world of women's golf had ever known by becoming the youngest player, the first foreigner and the first amateur to win the coveted title. Two years later she proved she was a really great player by winning both the British and American Amateur Championships. Also that year she won the French Open again and the Spanish Open, to record a remarkable Grand Slam. At the age of only 24 she retired from competitive golf to marry.

Had Miss Lacoste entered the professional ranks, who knows what fortune she would have amassed on the lucrative American tournament circuit? Nancy Lopez was only 20 when she turned professional in 1977 and ended the year as the top money winner with earnings of $189,813 – a record. This was even more than any man had achieved in his first year at that time, and playing in tournaments in Great Britain and Japan she did more to influence women's golf throughout the world than anyone before her. Still playing, she is one of the many women dollar millionaires playing golf in the United States. Women's professional golf in Europe is beginning to take off, and with the prize money now increasing to a worthwhile figure it is likely that great golfers will emerge to challenge the American supremacy. One such could be Laura Davies. This big-hitting English girl won the 1986 British Women's Open at Royal Birkdale, and the 1987 US Women's Open at Plainfield, New Jersey – the first ever British winner of the event.

These great golfers, with their different styles and personalities, all have one thing in common – none thought themselves greater than the game itself. This is why golf still remains the finest character-building sport in the world.

THE MAJOR CHAMPIONSHIPS

Greg Norman, 'The Awesome Aussie', holding the Open Championship trophy after his win at Turnberry in 1986.

RIGHT The 13th Earl of Eglington presented the Championship Belt for the first British Open, which was contested at Prestwick in 1860. The trophy was won by Willie Park of Musselburgh.

FAR RIGHT Young Tom Morris wearing the Championship Belt which he won outright, in 1870, after three Open Championship wins in a row.

The British Open, the United States Open, the US PGA and the US Masters are the four major championships that constitute the Grand Slam of golf. Only four golfers – Gene Sarazen, Ben Hogan, Jack Nicklaus and Gary Player – have won all four titles, but no one has ever won all four in the same year. The Australian, Greg Norman, led in all four going into the last round in 1986, but managed to win only one, the British Open at Turnberry.

Of these four championships the British Open is the oldest and is therefore generally regarded as the supreme championship. Played only on links (seaside) courses, which have the tightest fairways, the most punishing rough, the slickest greens and the strongest winds, the event is also regarded by the finest golfers in the world as the toughest of championships to win – the supreme test of their outstanding talents. Being the first in the field, the Open originally needed no prefix, and by custom even now when golfers refer to the Open they mean the British Open.

● THE OPEN ● CHAMPIONSHIP

The Open first saw the light of day at the then small and peaceful fishing town of Prestwick on the west coast of Scotland in the 19th century. At the suggestion of Major J O Fairlie, the secretary of the Prestwick Golf Club, the event first took place on 17 October, 1860, and was contested by eight professionals. The first winner of the red leather Championship Belt was Willie Park of Musselburgh, with a total of 174 for the three rounds played over what was then a 12-hole course. This is now generally accepted as the first Open Championship, but, strictly speaking, this is not quite correct. The contest of 1860 was staged for professionals only and therefore not an open competition in the true sense. However, the following year it was decided to open the Championship to 'all the world', which has been the situation ever since.

LEFT Taiwan's Liang Huan Lu, 'Mr Lu' to the crowds and everyone's favourite during the 1971 Open at Royal Birkdale, Southport, Merseyside.

ABOVE The Frenchman Arnaud Massy was the first overseas player to win the Open with his victory at Hoylake, the home of the Royal Liverpool Golf Club, in 1907.

When the Championship Belt was presented by the Earl of Eglington, it was agreed that anyone who won the title three times in succession would be allowed to keep the belt as his own property. This rule was responsible for the first of three interruptions (the others caused by World Wars I and II) that the event has suffered in its history. Young Tom Morris won three in a row from 1868 to 1870, and with no trophy to play for, the Championship was held in abeyance in 1871. The event was restarted in 1872 when the Royal and Ancient Golf Club of St Andrews and the Honourable Company of Edinburgh Golfers (then at Musselburgh) agreed to join Prestwick in subscribing to the purchase of a new trophy in the shape of a silver claret jug – a permanent trophy which the champion would retain for one year.

Nowadays, the precious trophy remains safely locked away and it is but a replica which is handed to each new champion to retain for a year. He also gets a gold medal, which is a keepsake. It was also agreed that the Championship would be staged by the three clubs in rotation.

The first man to win the new trophy was Young Tom Morris, a victory which gave him four Championships in a row – a record still unequalled. The Open continued to be played at the three clubs until 1892, when the Honourable Company moved from Musselburgh to Muirfield, where the tournament was hosted that year. In 1894 it was decided to introduce other venues into the rota, and Royal St George's, Sandwich, gained the distinction of becoming the first non-Scottish club to stage the Open Championship. Hoylake, the home of the Royal Liverpool Golf Club, became the second English club to enter the Championship rota when invited to stage the event in 1897, and there was cause for a double celebration because Harold Hilton, a member of the host club, upstaged the professionals to win the coveted title for the second time, having previously won at Muirfield in 1892. Earlier, in 1890, John Ball, also from the Royal Liverpool Club, had become the first amateur and the first Englishman to win the Open when it first took place at Prestwick.

The American Bobby Jones still remains the only other amateur to win the title (in 1926, 1927 and 1930) since the two Englishmen's victories in the last century. But the first time the Championship was won by an overseas player was at Hoylake in 1907 when Arnaud Massy, a Frenchman, held on to beat J H Taylor by two

strokes. The title went across the Atlantic for the first time in 1921 when Jock Hutchison, a Scotsman who had emigrated to the United States when a youngster, won after a play-off with the amateur, Roger Wethered, the brother of the great woman golfer, Joyce Wethered.

Before that, in 1919, at the suggestion of Mr Robert Maxwell of the Honourable Company, the Royal and Ancient Club took over the complete running of the Open, a task performed by their Championship Committee ever since. With Prestwick no longer considered a suitable venue because of its lack of length and limited space to accommodate the increasing volume of traffic, the centenary Open in 1960 was held, appropriately, at St Andrews, and was won by the Australian, Kel Nagle, who beat Arnold Palmer

TOP LEFT A classic 1920s photograph of Ted Ray, who won the US Open at Inverness, Ohio, in 1920.

ABOVE LEFT Ralph Guldahl, the first man to score four sub-par rounds in the US Open, in 1937, playing a perfect sand shot.

ABOVE The famous duel between Tom Watson and Jack Nicklaus during the 1977 Open at Turnberry, Strathclyde.

● THE US OPEN ●
CHAMPIONSHIP

Unlike the British Open, which has been played on only 14 links courses in its entire history, the United States Open Championship has been staged on both inland and coastal venues and the number of courses used will shortly pass the 50 mark. With a far greater land mass than Great Britain to cover in order to spread the Championship to all parts of the United States, the use of more courses is, of course, an understandable policy. The inaugural Championship took place at Newport, Rhode Island, in 1895, a day after the first United States Amateur Championship was played on the same course, and was won by a young Englishman named Horace Rawlins, an assistant professional at the host club, who scored 45, 46, 41, 41 in his four rounds on the nine-hole course.

British players who had emigrated to the United States dominated the event for a further

TOP Willie Anderson (bow tie), four times winner of the US Open, with Alex Smith (polo neck), who won the event twice. Sitting at their feet is Horace Rawlins, the first US Open champion with his victory at Newport, Rhode Island, in 1895.

ABOVE The immortal Bobby Jones (left) with the British and United States Open and Amateur trophies, which he won in the space of one year in 1930.

by one stroke. The actual 100th Open Championship took place at Royal Birkdale, Southport, in 1971 and was won by Lee Trevino after an epic struggle with the unknown Liang Huan Lu from Taiwan – dubbed Mr Lu by the appreciative crowds who warmed to his charming smile and politeness.

The Open, with its massive tented village accommodating hundreds of exhibition stands appertaining to golf, its huge media coverage and the entry of talented international golfers, competing in famous historic arenas for the ultimate prize of instant worldwide fame and fortune, is the greatest golf show on Earth. No other Championship attracts so many visitors from overseas, all wanting to soak in the atmosphere of the ancient game.

15 years, and during that time Harry Vardon added to the misery of the Americans by picking up the title during a promotional tour of the United States. The first American-born player to win the US Open was John J McDermott at Chicago, Illinois, in 1911 after a play-off with Mike Brady and George Simpson. The previous year McDermott, in the last year of his teens, had tied with the Smith brothers, Alex and Macdonald, only to lose to Alex in the play-off by six strokes while finishing ahead of Macdonald by two.

In 1912 McDermott successfully defended his title with an outright win after holding off a strong challenge from another American-born player, Thomas McNamara, who scored a 69 in the last round, having previously recorded the same score in the 1909 Open to become the first man to score below 70 in the Championship. Altogether McNamara finished three times in the runner-up position (1909, 1912 and 1915), but never once was he to win the great event. As for McDermott, he was forced to give up the game in 1915 because of a mental illness, thought by many at the time to have been sparked off by his obsessive determination to personally end the domination of the English and Scottish professionals who had emigrated to his country.

The last Briton to win the US Open was Tony Jacklin at the Hazeltine National, Chaska, Minnesota in 1970, when he led from start to finish and became only the second man to score four sub-par rounds in the event – Ralph Guldahl, an American from Dallas, Texas, being the first at Oakland Hills, Michigan, in 1937. Jacklin's winning margin of seven strokes was the widest since Jim Barnes won with 11 strokes to spare in 1921. The previous British winner before Jacklin's brilliant victory was Ted Ray in 1920 – a span of exactly 50 years. How different from the early days of the US Open!

Only four men – Willie Anderson, Bobby Jones, Ben Hogan and Jack Nicklaus – have managed to win the US Open four times, and Anderson's record of three wins in a row, beginning in 1903, has never been matched. The only amateur among these four is Bobby Jones, and he belongs to a select band of only five amateurs who have won the Championship; the others being Francis Ouimet in 1913, Jerome D Travers in 1915, Charles Evans in 1916 and Johnny Goodman in 1933.

Ouimet's victory in 1913 caused the biggest sensation by virtue of his play-off defeat of two-thirds of the Great Triumvirate, Harry Vardon and J H Taylor. Bobby Jones' fourth victory in the event in 1930 was also sensational, as it helped him achieve the then Grand Slam of the Open and Amateur titles of both the United States and Great Britain in the same year.

Another milestone in the tournament came at Bellerive, Mississippi, in 1965, when for the first time ever there was a play-off between two players who were born in neither Great Britain nor The United States. Gary Player of South Africa beat the Australian, Kel Nagle, and in doing so became the first overseas player outside Britain to win the US Open. The only overseas golfer, other than Jacklin, to take the trophy out of the United States since Player's historic victory is David Graham of Australia at Merion, Pennsylvania, in 1981, although Greg Norman, another Australian, came close at Winged Foot, New York, in 1984, losing only after a play-off with Fuzzy Zoeller.

Nowadays, unless one is an exempt player, attempting to qualify for one of the limited non-exempt places in the final field of 150 in the US Open is a costly and time-consuming exercise. Over 5,000 entries are now received by the USGA, and there is a long process of pre-qualifying and qualifying rounds at various venues to determine which handful of players gets into the main event. It is therefore not surprising that the US Open is now predominantly an all-American event. With only a remote chance of getting through, overseas players are not prepared to spend the time nor the money in trying.

Nevertheless, for those who make the grade, the prize money is surging toward the $1-million mark, and the winner is guaranteed much more than that from the fringe benefits which follow such a victory. The United States Open Championship has certainly come a long way since it was formed more or less as an afterthought by the United States Golf Association as an appendage to the National Amateur Championship in 1895. Although the tournament celebrates its Centenary in 1995, the two interruptions (1917-18 and 1942-45) because of the World Wars have unwittingly determined that the 100th US Open will be played in the year 2,000. To somebody will fall the historic distinction of becoming the 100th winner and the first of the 21st century.

● THE PROFESSIONAL ●
GOLFERS CHAMPIONSHIP

The Professional Golfers Championship of America, widely known as the US PGA, is the third in seniority among the four major championships. It was first held in 1916 at Siwanoy Country Club, New York, the same year that the Professional Golfers Association of America was formed. For the professional it is a most important event to win because each winner receives exemption for life from pre-qualifying for any of the PGA tournaments. This in itself is a great incentive for the players, who are naturally anxious to avoid strain and anguish of the strenuous pre-qualifying tournaments.

Jim Barnes was the first winner of the event, and because of World War I he had to wait three years before successfully defending his title. The following year (1920), Jock Hutchison, British-born like Barnes, emerged the victor. The first American-born player to record a victory in the event was Walter Hagen in 1921, a win which heralded a glorious chapter of PGA triumphs for the flamboyant American. In seven years he won the Championship five times – four of them in a row from 1924. Typical of Hagen, when his impressive run came to an end in 1928 he said he had not seen the trophy since 1925, but vaguely remembered leaving it in a taxi! However, when the time came to hand over the trophy to the new champion, Leo Diegel, it was in its proper place on the presentation stand. In those days the PGA was a matchplay event, and the cut and thrust of the knockout matches was ideally suited to Hagen's swashbuckling style of recovery play, which intimidated his opponents.

All the great players who were around when the Championship was matchplay won the event at least twice. Gene Sarazen and Sam Snead each won it three times, Byron Nelson and Ben Hogan twice. The only great name missing is that of Bobby Jones who, being an amateur, was barred from the tournament. However, with six former champions being beaten in the first two

ABOVE The 6th hole at the PGA National, Palm Beach, Florida. The home of the US PGA hosted the 1971 Championship which was won by Jack Nicklaus. This win gave Nicklaus the second of his PGA titles and made him the first man to win all four major championship titles twice.

rounds of the 1953 PGA at Birmingham, Michigan, the writing was on the wall for the Championship in its matchplay format. Television viewing was on the increase and demanded from golf the need not only for the game to be still in progress at peak viewing times, but also that the stars would be in action. Matchplay golf could not guarantee this, and in 1958 the tournament finally became strokeplay, decided over 72 holes.

Since changing to strokeplay the PGA title has eluded two great golfers, Arnold Palmer and Tom Watson. Palmer came close to winning on three occasions, only to finish the runner-up each time. The 1964 Championship at Columbus, Ohio, was particularly frustrating for him. Becoming the first player ever to score below 70 in all four rounds, he still finished in a tie for second place with Jack Nicklaus. Bobby Nichols, with a brilliant opening round of 64, won by three strokes and a record total of 271.

Gary Player, from South Africa, won at Aronimink, Pennsylvania, in 1962 to become the first overseas-based member of the Association to hold the title, which he regained at Oakland Hills, Michigan, in 1972. When the Championship was held for the first time at the PGA headquarters at Palm Beach, Florida, in 1971, it was rather fitting that Jack Nicklaus, the greatest golfer of all time, should win the second of his five PGA titles, thus becoming the first man to have won all four majors twice. An even more historic moment for Nicklaus came at Canterbury, Ohio, in 1973, when his third PGA victory saw him pass Bobby Jones' tally of 13 major titles, and at Oak Hills, New York, in 1980 he equalled Walter Hagen's outstanding record of five PGA titles.

The only Australian to have held the title is David Graham, who won at Oakland Hills in 1979 after a play-off with Ben Crenshaw. Graham's fellow countryman, the luckless Greg Norman, almost emulated him at Inverness, Ohio, in 1986, only to see the title escape from his grasp at the very last moment when Bob Tway holed out from a sand trap at the finishing hole. An equally memorable occasion was Lee Trevino's win in the battle of the 'Golden Oldies' at Shoal Greek, Alabama, in 1984, when he scored below 70 in every round. Gary Player incredibly tied for second place with the help of a 63 which equalled the lowest-ever round in the Championship set by Bruce Crampton in 1975. Trevino was then a 44-year-old and Player 49!

TOP The magnificent Masters trophy.

ABOVE Roberto de Vicenzo, the popular Argentinian golfer, lost the 1968 Masters title to Bob Goalby due to a scorecard error.

RIGHT At last a major title. Ben Crenshaw (right) proudly receives the traditional Masters green jacket from Seve Ballesteros after winning the 1984 Masters.

● THE MASTERS ●

The last, but certainly not least, of the four major championships is the United States Masters tournament. It is unique for a major in that it is always staged at the same venue, the Augusta National Club, Georgia. Other differences include the field being limited to about 75 competitors – half the size of that in the other majors – and the organizing committee reserving the right to invite whom they think fit, although most invitations are now guided by rules of qualification. Past champions have their own private locker room which no one else is allowed to enter unless invited, and each year before the tournament a past champions' dinner takes place, hosted by the reigning champion. Tradition also has it that the tournament winner becomes an honorary member of the Augusta National Club, and a ceremony is held whereby he receives the club's special green blazer into which he is helped by the immediate past champion. Amazingly, no matter the size of the new champion, the jacket is always the perfect fit. No advertising is allowed on the course and the programme is a single sheet of paper with just enough space for a map of the course, the starting times and a plea to the spectators not to applaud bad shots. Until 1987 it has been the policy not to announce the size of the prize money.

Bobby Jones founded the Masters in 1934 after having been responsible for creating the great golf course along with the golf architect, Alister Mackenzie, who had earlier designed Cypress Point, California. Previously the site had been owned by a Belgian, Baron Berckmans, and was called Fruitlands. Fittingly, Jones became the club president of Augusta National in perpetuity, and it was he who insisted on the highest standards for the tournament. When he died in 1971, Clifford Roberts, the club chairman, took over the running of the Masters, and he continued along the same traditional path as Jones. His successor, Bill Lane, who sadly died within two years of taking office, and the present incumbent, Hord Hardin, have been equally successful in maintaining the high standards set by Bobby Jones. Thankfully, the temptation to turn the Masters into a sponsors' money-making circus has been resisted and the tournament still retains its old-fashioned charm and sobriety.

Although Jones had retired from competitive golf four years prior to the staging of the first

RIGHT Jack Nicklaus being helped into his green jacket by Bernhard Langer after winning the Masters title for a record sixth time in 1986.

FAR RIGHT Germany's Bernhard Langer swinging his way to victory in the 1985 Masters at Augusta.

Masters tournament in 1934, he agreed to take part to help draw the crowds. Inviting many of the fine golfers he had competed against in the past, Jones managed to finish tied in 13th place; and the honour of winning the first Masters went to Horton Smith, with a four-round total of 284. The following year the tournament was firmly put on the golfing map after making front-page news in the national press. Gene Sarazen was the man responsible for this when he sensationally holed his four-wood second shot at the par five 15th for an unbelievable albatross (three below par) during the final round, which enabled him to tie with the leader in the clubhouse, Craig Wood.

The following day Sarazen won the 36-hole play-off, and the Masters has not looked back since. Incidentally, Wood had also been the runner-up in the inaugural Masters, but he finally won the tournament in 1941.

Byron Nelson, who had won the title in 1937, was again the champion in 1942 – this year the tournament was suspended for the duration of World War II. Jimmy Demaret's victory in 1950 gave him the distinction of becoming the first man to win the Masters three times, and four years later Sam Snead equalled the record. Although a sprinkling of amateurs is invited to play each year, no amateur has yet managed to gain immortal fame by winning the coveted title; but Frank Stranahan in 1947, Ken Venturi in 1956 and Charlie Coe in 1961 all finished in second place. The Big Three – Arnold Palmer, Jack Nicklaus and Gary Player – dominated the event for nine years from 1958. During this period Palmer won four times, Nicklaus three times and Player once. Player's triumph in 1961 saw him become the first non-American to hold the title. However, the famous trio did not feature in the winners' list again until 1972, when Palmer's record of four victories was equalled by Nicklaus. Player won again in 1974 and 1978.

Without a doubt, the saddest year in the history of the Masters was 1968. Millions of television viewers witnessed the joy on the face of Roberto de Vicenzo, the popular Argentinian player, as he walked off the final green having forced a play-off with Bob Goalby. Vicenzo's joy, however, was short-lived when it was discovered that in his excitement he had failed to notice a four marked on his card for the 17th hole where, in fact, he had scored three. Having signed the scorecard as correct, the four had to stand under the rules. Therefore, Goalby was declared the winner and the luckless Vicenzo the runner-up. In the true spirit of the game Vicenzo graciously accepted the decision as correct and did his best to console his partner, Tommy Aaron, who had inadvertently marked the incorrect score on the Argentinian's card. For his sportsmanship Vicenzo was awarded the Bobby Jones Award in 1970.

Such are the pressures of this great tournament, that no man had ever won the Masters at his first attempt until the fun-loving, easy-going Fuzzy Zoeller won after a play-off with Tom Watson and Ed Sneed in 1979. In 1980 Severiano Ballesteros, fresh from his British Open victory in 1979, became the youngest man to win the title at the age of 23 – beating Nicklaus' record, achieved in 1963, by a couple of months. Ballesteros won again in 1983, but the title went the following year to the American most people wanted to see win – Ben Crenshaw. A great lover of the history and traditions of the game, and a keen collector of golfing relics, the likeable Texan's burning desire to win a major title looked doomed to failure after many near misses. Crenshaw had been runner-up three times in the Masters, twice in the British Open, once in the PGA and had tied for third place in the US Open. At last, with the crowd willing him home, his putter worked like a magic wand in the final round and he won with two strokes to spare over Tom Watson. A memorable moment for the proud young man known by all as Gentle Ben.

Bernhard Langer's win in 1985 made him the first German to win any major golf championship. The son of a Bavarian bricklayer, Langer has had a great influence on golf in Germany, and golf courses are springing up in all parts of West Germany as more and more people take up the sport.

In the Masters of 1986 Jack Nicklaus proved that age is no barrier to winning tournaments, providing one has the talent and stamina. At the age of 46 he won the masters for a record sixth time, notching his 18th major championship win in all. It is little wonder that Bobby Jones once remarked of Nicklaus: 'He plays a game with which I am not familiar'.

Greg Norman, the highly talented Australian, has good cause to remember that particular tournament, for had he not sent his approach shot to the final hole into the crowd, it might have been his triumph. Again, in 1987, Norman stood on the threshold of a Masters victory only to have it snatched from his grasp. Involved in a three-man sudden-death play-off with Ballesteros and Larry Mize, which had seen the Spaniard eliminated at the first extra hole, Norman looked home and dry at the very next hole. Mize, however, chipped in for an unlikely birdie three and the Awesome Aussie was deprived of yet another major title.

INTERNATIONAL
TEAM COMPETITIONS

An historic occasion. The 1987 European Ryder Cup
team after gaining a first-ever win on American soil.

Had not an unofficial match between members of the United States and the British Professional Golfers Associations taken place at Wentworth, Surrey, in 1926, there might never have been a Ryder Cup. The fact that the British team won so convincingly by 13½ points to 1½ made little impact on the British public, and only a handful of people thought it worthwhile to go along to watch. People in the Britain of 1926 had more important issues to occupy their minds than a mere game of golf, for this was the year of the National Strike – and life was at a standstill. But among the small crowd who witnessed the staggering victory by the British team was one Samuel Ryder, a wealthy Englishman who had made his fortune selling inexpensive packets of seeds. The match left a lasting impression on him, so much so that the following year he donated a magnificent trophy made of solid gold to be contested for biennially by the two great golfing nations.

• THE RYDER CUP •

Played alternately in Great Britain and the United States, the first Ryder Cup match took place at Worcester, Massachusetts, in June 1927. The Americans gained ample revenge for their unofficial defeat of 1926 by thrashing the British team 9½ points to 2½. Honours remained even after the first four encounters – each side winning the trophy when playing on home soil. The pattern, however, changed dramatically as the years went by. From the time the British team scraped to a narrow victory by 6½ points to 5½ when Syd Easterbrook sunk his vital putt at Southport and Ainsdale, Lancashire, in 1933 to defeat Densmore Shute in the last game, the Americans remained undefeated until 1957. Then a rare British victory proved but a minor setback in the American domination of the series. In 1961, at Royal Lytham and St Annes, Lancashire, an attempt was made to make the series more interesting by changing the format with matches being reduced from 36 holes to

FAR LEFT Harry Vardon, J H Taylor, Sandy Herd and James Braid flank Samuel Ryder (centre), the wealthy Englishman who donated the wonderful solid-gold trophy (below far left) in 1927.

LEFT Massed crowds surround the first hole for the 1985 Ryder Cup at the Belfry, England.

RIGHT 1987 Open Champion Nick Faldo in Ryder Cup action at Muirfield Village, Ohio.

PAGE 84 (see over) The triumphant 1987 US Walker Cup team at Sunningdale, England. The United States have been victorious in all but two of their encounters with Britain and Ireland since the inauguration of the Walker Cup in 1922.

PAGE 85 (see over) The Walker Cup trophy.

18. This only resulted in more matches, and more points at stake, and thus emphasized the superiority of the Americans, who went on to win by 14½ to 9½.

The encounter at Atlanta, Georgia, in 1963 saw a further change made in the format. Four-ball matches and an extra day were introduced for the first time, but this merely meant the British suffering humiliation on a much wider scale — crushed by 23 points to 9. Nevertheless, America's stranglehold on the series was forced to relax slightly when, at Royal Birkdale, in 1969, a British team, no doubt inspired by Tony Jacklin's Open Championship triumph earlier that year, forced a most memorable draw. With the teams level and Jacklin in the very last match needing to hole his two-foot putt on the 18th green to prevent the United States team winning yet again, Jack Nicklaus, with a heart-warming show of sportsmanship, conceded the putt by picking up Jacklin's ball, and the match was tied 16–16. This was the first drawn match in the history of the Ryder Cup and each country held the trophy for 12 months. Unknown to anyone at that time, a solely British team was never again to get nearer to beating the powerful Americans.

Defeat followed defeat, which led to a decision being made in 1979 whereby the team to

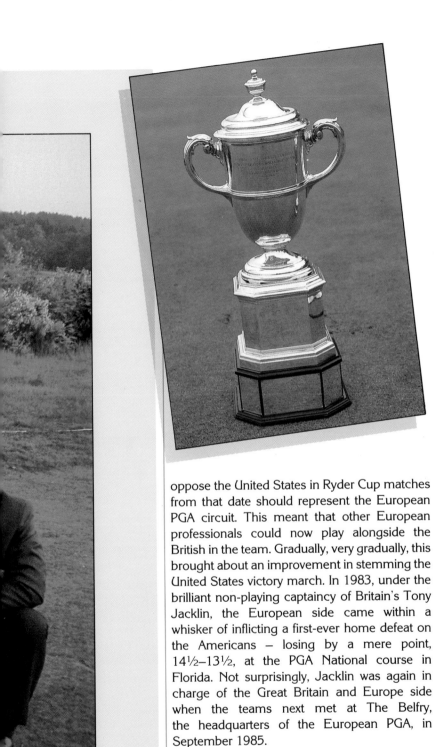

oppose the United States in Ryder Cup matches from that date should represent the European PGA circuit. This meant that other European professionals could now play alongside the British in the team. Gradually, very gradually, this brought about an improvement in stemming the United States victory march. In 1983, under the brilliant non-playing captaincy of Britain's Tony Jacklin, the European side came within a whisker of inflicting a first-ever home defeat on the Americans – losing by a mere point, 14½–13½, at the PGA National course in Florida. Not surprisingly, Jacklin was again in charge of the Great Britain and Europe side when the teams next met at The Belfry, the headquarters of the European PGA, in September 1985.

The atmosphere was electric on the final day as the European team, which included the Open champion, Sandy Lyle, the Masters champion, Bernhard Langer, and Severiano Ballesteros, the world's number one golfer at that time, ended the American domination by 16½ points to 11½ – the first American defeat for 28 years. In 1987, the European team, again captained by Tony Jacklin, retained the title with a 15–13 victory, and added a new chapter to the history of the Ryder Cup with a first-ever win on US soil.

● THE WALKER CUP ●

Like the Ryder Cup, the Walker Cup series began as a result of an unofficial match played between teams of American and British golfers. Unlike the Ryder Cup, however, the Walker Cup is for competition between teams of amateurs. The unofficial match took place on the day before the British Amateur Championship at Royal Liverpool, Hoylake, in 1921. Earlier that same year the United States Golf Association had sent invitations to all golfing nations to send teams to compete for the Walker Cup, donated by George Herbert Walker, the president of the USGA. For various reasons they all declined the invitation, but following the 1921 match the Royal and Ancient Club sent a British team to America in 1922 to play the United States for the trophy at the National Links, Long Island, the home club of George H Walker. The Americans won that match and the next two at St Andrews and Garden City, New York, in 1923 and 1924 respectively. Since then the match has been biennial with the United States dominating the series.

Of all the notable amateurs who have played in the Walker Cup, Bobby Jones had a particularly fine record. In his four appearances between 1924 and 1930, he was unbeatable in his singles matches, winning them all by wide margins, and in the foursomes he lost only once.

Leonard Crawley, one of the great characters of British golf, literally made his mark on the Walker Cup at the Country Club, Brookline, Massachusetts, in 1932 when his approach shot to the 18th green overshot and struck the famous trophy, which was out on display awaiting the presentation ceremony, a fierce metal-denting blow.

An even more remarkable incident happened in the inaugural meeting on Long Island. The British team of eight players was not covered by reserves, and when Robert Harris, the captain, withdrew because of illness before the match, his place as captain and player was taken by Bernard Darwin, the doyen of golf writers, who was covering the match for *The Times* newspaper. Although losing in the foursomes when playing with Cyril Tolley, Darwin, an English international golfer of note, played a captain's part in the singles by beating the American captain, William Fownes.

Despite the fact that the United States won 27 of the first 30 matches played, the appeal of the Walker Cup has never waned, and golfers of both countries regard being selected as the highest honour of their career. Both British victories, in 1938 and 1971, took place at St Andrews, but they would dearly like the next one to be on American soil. The nearest they have come to achieving this was in Baltimore, Maryland, in 1965 when, having led 10–4 with eight games left to play, Clive Clark was left with the daunting task of sinking his 35-foot putt on the 18th green to halve his match and save his country from yet another defeat. Clark's attempt was successful and Britain managed to escape with a 12–12 draw.

• THE CURTIS CUP •

Unofficial international matches between the women golfers of the United States and Great Britain were played long before their male counterparts took up the idea. Indeed, the women's matches go back as far as 1905, when an American team challenged the British to a match on the eve of the British Women's Amateur Championship at Cromer, Norfolk. In-

cluded in the American team were the sisters Margaret and Harriot Curtis, who were both destined to win the US Women's Amateur Championship twice. A number of these unofficial matches took place in later years, and the match at Sunningdale in 1930 created a great deal of interest on both sides of the Atlantic. This prompted the sisters to present a trophy for a regular biennial contest between the US and British women's teams – and thus was born the Curtis Cup.

The first match took place at Wentworth, Surrey, in 1932 and, like the Ryder Cup and the Walker Cup, the series has been dominated by the United States. With victory going to the Americans by 5½ matches to 3½ in the inaugural match, Britain had to wait until 1952 to record their first win, at Muirfield, Scotland, although they had forced a draw at Gleneagles, Scotland, in 1936. Four years later, at Prince's, Kent, they won again, and in the very next encounter they all but brought off a sensational result on American soil at Brae Burn, Massachusetts, where they tied 4½–4½. The British, however, lost the next home match in 1960 at Lindrick, Yorkshire, by 6½ points to 2½, and the Americans continued on their victory trail for the next 24 years.

The 1984 match at Muirfield gave an indication of better things to come for the British who, fighting hard for every point, lost only by 9½–8½. And so it proved at Prairie Dunes, Kansas, in 1986 when the British team, against all odds, made golfing history by becoming the first team ever, male or female, to bring about the downfall of an American team on American soil. With three of their 1984 team lost to the professional ranks, the British selectors made a bold gamble in bringing back Belle Robertson who, aged 50, became the oldest ever to take an active part in the Curtis Cup. Jill Thornhill, 44, retained her place and three young players, Patricia (Trish) Johnson, Karen Davies and Lilian Behan, were making their debut. As far as the pundits were concerned this was a team of no-hopers, but they reckoned without Diane Bailey, the determined non-playing captain whom the selectors had kept faith with after the near miss of 1984. She was in charge of a team which contained a blend of youth and experience and knew exactly the mix needed to produce a successful recipe. At the end of two unbelievable days the British achieved an astonishing result – winning by 13 points to 5.

THE GREAT
COURSES OF THE WORLD

Players on the 18th green at Pebble Beach, California,
with Monterey Bay in the background.

one of the famous golf clubs, can tread the hallowed fairways to their heart's content. Even the casual visitors, provided they are playing members of another club, have the opportunity to pay a moderate fee to play a round at most of the tournament venues dotted round the world.

● AUGUSTA NATIONAL ●

The Augusta National, Georgia, is unquestionably one of the greatest and most beautiful inland golf courses in the world. The home of the Masters tournament, it was designed by the immortal Bobby Jones and the eminent Scottish golf architect, Alister Mackenzie, in the early 1930s on land that was once a horticultural nursery. A staggering 7,030 yards (6,427 m) in length, with a par of 72, each of its 18 holes is unique in being named after flora: for example, Flowering Peach is the third, Yellow Jasmine the eighth and Golden Bell the twelfth. The best time to visit Augusta is in the spring when the plants and shrubs are ablaze with glorious colour, giving forth an atmosphere of calm and serenity. Should you be one of the fortunate few invited to play at Augusta, concentrate on keeping both eyes on the ball at address, otherwise you could be heading for trouble as a result of your eagerness to take in the majestic scenery. A famous part of the course is Amen corner, which takes in the eleventh to thirteenth holes, all with water close to the green and notorious for ruining the chances of many players during the Masters.

An exclusive club with a membership of around 250, the National in the title was included because the intention was – and still is – that members should be drawn from all parts of the United States, and some from overseas, from where currently there are about 15 members. But the most notable member was President Dwight Eisenhower who, during his visits lived in a large white bungalow, called Mamie's Cabin after his wife, on the fringe of the tenth hole.

During World War II the course was completely closed and cattle were allowed to graze there. However, after a short time they were removed because of the damage caused to the greens and rare shrubs, and, instead, the course became a turkey farm. Nevertheless by 1946 the celebrated course was restored to its original splendour, and gets better and better as the years go by.

ABOVE An example of the beautiful flora to be seen at Augusta National, Georgia. The course, designed by Alister Mackenzie and Bobby Jones, was originally a horticultural nursery.

RIGHT Augusta National during the 1987 Masters tournament.

One of the most fascinating things about golf is that the ordinary everyday golfer who plays the game merely as a pastime, without any thought of reward or lasting fame, is able, should he wish, to play on the actual famous arenas used by the stars. What would a tennis fan give to be allowed to play on the Centre Court at Wimbledon, the cricket fan at Lords or the American football fan at the Superbowl stadium? Yet golfers, should they be lucky enough to be members of

● ST ANDREWS ●

The most famous golf course in the world is the Old Course at St Andrews, Scotland. The home of the Royal and Ancient Club, it is steeped in the history of golf and has long been regarded as its Mecca. It is the dream of golfers from all parts of the globe to play the Old Course at least once in their lifetime and to soak in the atmosphere of the grand old place, which has been the venue of the Open Championship on no less than 23 occasions. Amazingly, it is a public course, owned by the Fife District Council, run jointly by the R and A and the Council through the St Andrew Links Trust and a management committee.

The first recorded evidence of golf being played at St Andrews dates back to 1552, and in 1873 it staged its first Open Championship. Try as you may, you will not find the name of the architect because it was nature and not man who fashioned the ancient links – man simply added the tees, shaped the treacherous bunkers from the natural land and manicured the greens. The course is sited on a narrow tract of land and goes straight out and back again by means of a loop, which takes in four holes (from the eighth to the eleventh) as the player turns back on his tracks for home. This famous loop, caused by accident rather than design, makes the shape of the course not unlike a golf club or maybe a hockey stick.

A feature of the Old Course is its enormous double greens and wide fairways which are shared by 14 of the holes on the outward and homeward journeys. The only holes with greens of their own are the first, ninth, seventeenth and eighteenth. As far as ease of walking is concerned it is essentially a flat course, but for players its endless humps, bumps and undulations, added to huge ball-gathering bunkers, make it one of the greatest tests of golf anywhere in the world. All in all it measures almost 7,000 yards (6,400 m) of pure delight or dismal dejection for the golfer, depending on the strength of the wind blowing in from St Andrews Bay. When Bobby Jones first played the Old Course, in 1921, he became so frustrated with his inability to come to terms with its subtleties that he tore his card up on the eleventh hole of his fourth round in the Open Championship.

The landmarks dotted round the course are world famous. The infamous Swilcan burn (stream), which wends its way across the first

LEFT St Andrews, Scotland, with a view of the 18th green and the 19th-century clubhouse.

TOP AND ABOVE These details of a 1920s plan of St Andrews' Old Course, clearly show the famous loop (top), and the broad double greens and fearful bunkers (above).

and eighteenth fairways, has brought the ambitions of many to a halt during the Open. Another ambition wrecker is the fourteenth hole with its five feared bunkers known as the Beardies' and also the aptly named Hell bunker. Bordering the eighteenth hole are the sombre old clubhouse, which was opened in 1854, and Old Tom Morris' golf shop. All the holes on the Old Course each carry a distinctive name: the Ginger Beer (fourth) was named after a ginger beer stall which stood alongside its fairway during the 19th century. Of interest to visiting Americans will be the Bobby Jones' tenth hole, named as a tribute to the great American amateur whom many rate the finest golfer ever.

A measure of the number of golfers, from all over the world, who make the pilgrimage to St Andrews can be taken from the fact that some 43,000 rounds are played on the Old Course each year. With so much traffic it is now deemed necessary for the course to be completely closed for one month, usually in the early spring, for a much-needed rest.

● WINGED FOOT ●

ABOVE Tommy Armour, photographed in 1932, taught golf at Winged Foot following his retirement from competitive golf.

Another famous American inland championship venue is Winged Foot, Mamaroneck, New York, which boasts two outstanding courses – the West and the East. The West is the most celebrated of the two because it has staged the US Open on four occasions, the first in 1929 when Bobby Jones won after a play-off with Al Espinosa, and the last in 1984, which saw Fuzzy Zoeller the winner after a play-off against Greg Norman.

The place derives it unusual name from the emblem of the New York Athletic Club, some of whose members founded the golf club. Designed in the early 1920s by A W Tillinghast, the creator of many wonderful courses in the United States, the West Course is notorious for its challenging finish which, spanning five of the longest par-four holes, collectively, in the world, always guarantees an exciting climax to the US Open when it is staged at Winged Foot. Indeed, before Zoeller and Norman tied on 276 – four under par for the four rounds – during the 1984 US Open, nobody had ever beaten par over four rounds of the event.

It is a well-known fact that tough courses produce fine players, and Winged Foot is no exception. Craig Wood was the professional there when he achieved his great double in 1941 by winning the Masters and US Open titles. Claude Harmon, who succeeded Wood, also won the Masters title in 1948. Dick Mayer, who played much of his amateur golf at Winged Foot before turning professional, became the US Open champion in 1957, while Jackie Burke, Dave Marr and Mike Souchak, among others, went on to find fame after honing their game on the West course when young assistant professionals at Winged Foot.

Tommy Armour, the great Scots character who took out American citizenship before going on to win the US Open in 1927, the US PGA in 1930 and the British Open in 1931, taught golf at Winged Foot for several years after ending his playing days. Among the many famous people who came to him for advice was President Nixon.

● PEBBLE BEACH ●

One of the most spectacular and toughest golf courses in the world is Pebble Beach, California. Situated alongside the rugged shoreline and cliffs of Carmel Bay, Pebble Beach has some truly magnificent seaside holes within its 6,825-yards (6,240-m), par 72, length. Indeed, the seven-hole stretch from the fourth to the tenth is rated by many as being the most beautiful yet most severe sequence of holes to be found at any championship venue. Of these the toughest are the last three. After the uphill tee shot at the par-four eighth, the second shot has to carry some 190 yards (174 m) across a bay to a well-bunkered tiny green. The ninth and tenth, also par fours, are equally demanding with fairways which slope toward the edge of the cliff, where the greens are cunningly placed.

As if this is not enough to test the best, Pebble Beach has a vicious sting in its tail in the shape of the seventeenth and eighteenth holes. After the course turns inland for six relatively easy holes from the eleventh to the sixteenth, these two splendid seaside finishing holes spell danger with a capital 'D'. The eighteenth, in particular, is an awesome hole with all of its 548 yards (501 m) fringing the beckoning cliffs. However, apparently because it is not in close proximity to a major city, the United States Open Championship has been held at Pebble Beach only twice (1972 and 1982).

FAR LEFT The clubhouse at Winged Foot, Marmaroneck, New York, as it was in the 1920s.

ABOVE The short, but challenging, 7th hole at Pebble Beach, California.

ABOVE The 5th hole at Muirfield, Scotland. Generally considered to be the fairest of linksland courses, Muirfield was also honoured when Jack Nicklaus named his first course design, in Dublin, Ohio, Muirfield Village.

● MUIRFIELD ●

Muirfield, the home of the Honourable Company of Edinburgh Golfers, ranks second in the list of famous golf courses which continue to stage the Open Championship. In July 1987 it staged the great event for the thirteenth time – the first being in 1892 when the amateur Harold Hilton won. In the same year, 1892, the Championship was extended from 36 to 72 holes. With a length of 6,926 yards (6,333 m), par 71, it lies on the edge of the Firth of Forth estuary, in East Lothian, Scotland, and like all the Open Championship courses it is a linksland course. Its design is such that it has an outer loop and an inner loop each consisting of nine holes, and each starting and finishing in close proximity to the famous Muirfield clubhouse. Indeed, it was one of the earliest (1891) courses in the world to use this type of design concept.

Muirfield is a particularly favoured course of many great golfers. Jack Nicklaus holds it in high esteem, and regards it as the best and fairest championship course in the British Isles.

• THE ROYAL MONTREAL •
CLUB

The Royal Montreal Club takes a special place in golfing history because it is the oldest constituted club, not only in Canada but on the North American continent. Having been granted permission in 1884 by Queen Victoria to use the 'Royal' prefix, the club celebrated its centenary in unique style in 1973 when teams from every 'Royal' club throughout the world were invited to take part in a special centenary competition.

The club's first site was at Fletcher's Field, a public park on the Mount Royal slopes, but in 1896 the club moved to a more suitable site at Dixie, on the outskirts of the city, where it stayed for 63 years until forced to move because of urban development. In 1959 the club moved to its present home on Ile Bizard in the Lake of Two Mountains. Today the club boasts two magnificent 18-hole championship courses and a splendid nine-hole course. Of these, the most famous is the Blue course, which is renowned as the finest golf course in Canada. A feature is the huge greens — almost double the usual size — and the four finishing holes with their vast expanses of water to negotiate. The sixteenth is an awesome hole. The tee shot is across a lake to a narrow fairway, and for the approach shot to the green the lake has to be recrossed at its widest point.

The Blue and the Red courses both have a par of 70, and when the Canadian Open was held on the 6,487 yards (5,929 m) Blue course in 1975, both Tom Weiskopf and Jack Nicklaus broke the course record in the opening round by three shots by scoring 65s. Weiskopf went on to win the title in a sudden death play-off.

ABOVE This photograph records the first international match between Canada and the United States, played in 1898 between The Country Club and Royal Montreal.

Nicklaus won his first Open title at Muirfield, and is among such greats as Vardon, Braid, Hagen, Cotton, Player, Trevino and Watson who have won the coveted title there. When he designed his first golf course, at Dublin, Ohio, Nicklaus named it Muirfield Village, as a mark of respect for the famous Scottish course. Part of Muirfield's attraction is that, except for the 11th, there are no blind holes, and all the many hazards are where they can be seen from the tee.

Yes, Muirfield, along with St Andrews, is a must in every golfers' itinerary when visiting Scotland.

TOP Royal Melbourne, the oldest golf club in Australia, was founded in 1891.

ABOVE A calm day at Portmarnock, Eire.

● ROYAL MELBOURNE ●

Royal Melbourne Golf Club is the oldest golf club in Australia. Founded in 1891, the club's first course was built on land near Caulfield Station, and opened on 4 July, 1891. However, as the century moved toward its close, Caulfield was required for building land and the club was forced to search for a new home. An area at Sandringham, near the sea, was chosen and the Lieutenant Governor, Sir John Madden, opened the new course in 1901.

Over the years the course built up a reputation as Australia's premier golf course, and today the club boasts two outstanding courses – the East and the West. When championships are held at Royal Melbourne a composite course – using the best holes of the East and West – provides a testing challenge for golfers of the highest skill. The rich soil of the sand belt, left behind by the receding sea, has proved an excellent growing medium for fairways and greens among the best in the world. A notable feature of Royal Melbourne is the massive sand bunkers carved out of the natural sandy soil. The length of the composite course is 6,946 yards (6,371 m) with a par of 71. Other oustanding championship golf courses in Australia are Royal Sydney and Royal Adelaide.

● PORTMARNOCK ●

A chapter on famous golf courses would be incomplete without a mention of the many outstanding courses which are to be found in the fair country of Ireland. Ballybunnion (what a splendid name for a golf course), Killarney, Royal County Down and Royal Portrush are all courses of the highest quality and all are set in romantic surroundings. But it is Portmarnock which is generally considered to be Ireland's greatest golf course. Situated some ten miles (16 km) from Dublin, Portmarnock, built in 1893, lies on pure linksland jutting out between the Irish Sea and an inland tidal bay. Surrounded on three sides by the sea, if offers 7,103 yards (6,494 m) of challenging golf when the prevailing so'westerly wind blows at full strength. However, when all is calm and the summer sun shines, it is an enchanting place to be.

Not surprisingly, Portmarnock has staged a number of important tournaments, which include the Irish Open, the Canada Cup, the Dunlop Masters and the British Amateur. For many years the only access to this delightful course was by crossing the estuary in a rowing boat or, at low tide, by pony and trap. Thankfully, there is now a main road passing by at the far end of the peninsula, and the course is linked to this by a track which borders the seventeenth and eighteenth holes.

These, then, are but eight of the great championship venues of the game of golf. There are many many others, each with their own special niche in the history of the glorious game which, throughout the centuries, has brought much enjoyment to countless millions of people of all ages and nationalities.

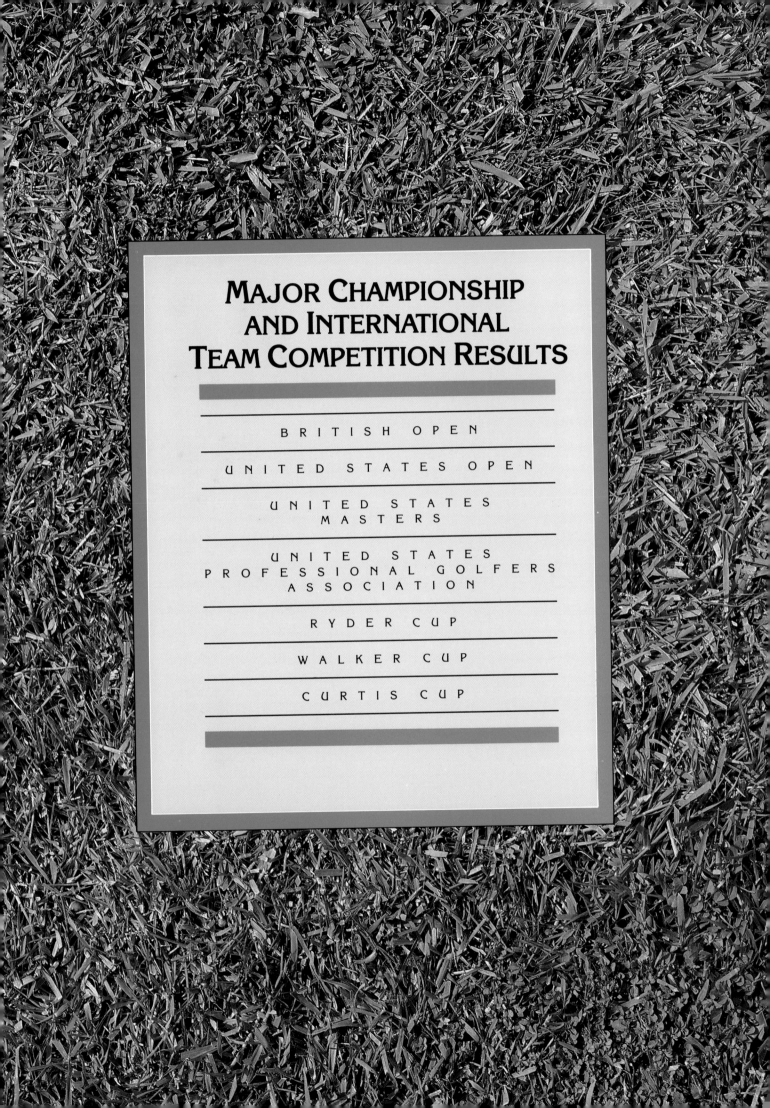

MAJOR CHAMPIONSHIP AND INTERNATIONAL TEAM COMPETITION RESULTS

BRITISH OPEN

UNITED STATES OPEN

UNITED STATES
MASTERS

UNITED STATES
PROFESSIONAL GOLFERS
ASSOCIATION

RYDER CUP

WALKER CUP

CURTIS CUP

BRITISH OPEN

YEAR	WINNER	VENUE	SCORE	YEAR	WINNER	VENUE	SCORE
1860	W. Park	Prestwick	174	1924	W. Hagen	Hoylake	301
1861	T. Morris Sen.	Prestwick	163	1925	J. Barnes	Prestwick	300
1862	T. Morris Sen.	Prestwick	163	1926	R. Jones (Am)	Lytham	291
1863	W. Park	Prestwick	168	1927	R. Jones (Am)	St. Andrews	285
1864	T. Morris Sen.	Prestwick	167	1928	W. Hagen	Sandwich	292
1865	A. Strath	Prestwick	162	1929	W. Hagen	Muirfield	292
1866	W. Park	Prestwick	169	1930	R. Jones (Am)	Hoylake	291
1867	T. Morris Sen.	Prestwick	170	1931	T. Armour	Carnoustie	296
1868	T. Morris Jr.	Prestwick	157	1932	G. Sarazen	Prince's	283
1869	T. Morris Jr.	Prestwick	154	1933	D. Shute	St. Andrews	292
1870	T. Morris Jr.	Prestwick	149	1934	T. H. Cotton	Sandwich	283
1871	No Championship			1935	A. Perry	Muirfield	283
1872	T. Morris Jr.	Prestwick	166	1936	A. H. Padgham	Hoylake	287
1873	T. Kidd	St. Andrews	179	1937	T. H. Cotton	Carnoustie	290
1874	M. Park	Musselburgh	159	1938	R. Whitecombe	Sandwich	295
1875	W. Park	Prestwick	166	1939	R. Burton	St. Andrews	290
1876	B. Martin	St. Andrews	176	1940–1945 No Championship			
1877	J. Anderson	Musselburgh	160				
1878	J. Anderson	Prestwick	157	1946	S. Snead	St. Andrews	290
1879	J. Anderson	St. Andrews	169	1947	F. Daly	Hoylake	293
1880	B. Ferguson	Musselburgh	162	1948	T. H. Cotton	Muirfield	284
1881	B. Ferguson	Prestwick	170	1949	A. D. Locke	Sandwich	283
1882	B. Ferguson	St. Andrews	171	1950	A. D. Locke	Troon	279
1883	W. Fernie	Musselburgh	159	1951	M. Faulkner	Ry. Portrush	285
1884	J. Simpson	Prestwick	160	1952	A. D. Locke	Ry. Lytha.n	287
1885	B. Martin	St. Andrews	171	1953	B. Hogan	Carnoustie	282
1886	D. Brown	Musselburgh	157	1954	P. Thomson	Ry. Birkdale	283
1887	W. Park Jr.	Prestwick	161	1955	P. Thomson	St. Andrews	281
1888	J. Burns	St. Andrews	171	1956	P. Thomson	Hoylake	286
1889	W. Park Jr.	Musselburgh	155	1957	A. D. Locke	St. Andrews	279
1890	J. Ball (Am)	Prestwick	164	1958	P. Thomson	Hoylake	278
1891	H. Kirkaldy	St. Andrews	166	1959	G. Player	Muirfield	284
1892	H. Hilton (Am)	Muirfield	305	1960	K. Nagle	St. Andrews	278
1893	W. Auchterlonie	Prestwick	322	1961	A. Palmer	Ry. Birkdale	284
1894	J. H. Taylor	Sandwich	326	1962	A. Palmer	Troon	276
1895	J. H. Taylor	St. Andrews	322	1963	R. J. Charles	Ry. Lytham	277
1896	H. Vardon	Muirfield	316	1964	A. Lema	St. Andrews	279
1897	H. Hilton (Am)	Hoylake	314	1965	P. Thomson	Ry. Birkdale	285
1898	H. Vardon	Prestwick	307	1966	J. Nicklaus	Muirfield	282
1899	H. Vardon	Sandwich	310	1967	R. de Vicenzo	Hoylake	278
1900	J. H. Taylor	St. Andrews	309	1968	G. Player	Carnoustie	289
1901	J. Braid	Muirfield	318	1969	A. Jacklin	Ry. Lytham	280
1902	A. Herd	Hoylake	307	1970	J. Nicklaus	St. Andews	283
1903	H. Vardon	Prestwick	300	1971	L. Trevino	Ry. Birkdale	278
1904	J. White	Sandwich	296	1972	L. Trevino	Muirfield	278
1905	J. Braid	St. Andrews	318	1973	T. Weiskopf	Troon	276
1906	J. Braid	Muirfield	300	1974	G. Player	Ry. Lytham	282
1907	A. Massy	Hoylake	312	1975	T. Watson	Carnoustie	279
1908	J. Braid	Prestwick	291	1976	J. Miller	Ry. Birkdale	279
1909	J. H. Taylor	Deal	295	1977	T. Watson	Turnberry	268
1910	J. Braid	St. Andrews	299	1978	J. Nicklaus	St. Andrews	281
1911	H. Vardon	Sandwich	303	1979	S. Ballesteros	Ry. Lytham	283
1912	E. Ray	Muirfield	295	1980	T. Watson	Muirfield	271
1913	J. H. Taylor	Hoylake	304	1981	W. Rogers	Ry. St. George's	276
1914	H. Vardon	Prestwick	306	1982	T. Watson	Ry. Troon	271
1915–1919 No Championship				1983	T. Watson	Ry. Birkdale	275
1920	G. Duncan	Deal	303	1984	S. Ballesteros	St. Andrews	276
1921	J. Hutchison	St. Andrews	296	1985	S. Lyle	Ry. St. George's	282
1922	W. Hagen	Sandwich	300	1986	G. Norman	Turnberry	280
1923	A. G. Havers	Troon	295	1987	N. Faldo	Muirfield	279

U.S. MASTERS TOURNAMENT
ALWAYS PLAYED AT AUGUSTA NATIONAL

YEAR	WINNER	SCORE
1934	Horton Smith	284
1935	Gene Sarazen	282
1936	Horton Smith	285
1937	Byron Nelson	283
1938	Henry Picard	285
1939	Ralph Guldahl	279
1940	Jim Demaret	280
1941	Craig Wood	280
1942	Byron Nelson	280
1943–1945 No Tournament		
1946	Herman Keiser	282
1947	Jim Demaret	281
1948	Cld. Harmon	279
1949	Sam Snead	282
1950	Jim Demaret	283
1951	Ben Hogan	280
1952	San Snead	286
1953	Ben Hogan	274
1954	San Snead	289
1955	Cary Middlecoff	279
1956	Jack Burke Jr.	289
1957	Doug Ford	282
1958	Arnold Palmer	284
1959	Art Wall Jr.	284
1960	Arnold Palmer	282
1961	Gary Player	280
1962	Arnold Palmer	280
1963	Jack Nicklaus	286
1964	Arnold Palmer	276
1965	Jack Nicklaus	271
1966	Jack Nicklaus	288
1967	Gary Brewer Jr.	280
1968	Bob Goalby	277
1969	George Archer	281
1970	Billy Casper	279
1971	Chas Coody	279
1972	Jack Nicklaus	286
1973	Tommy Aaron	283
1974	Gary Player	278
1975	Jack Nicklaus	276
1976	Ray Floyd	271
1977	Tom Watson	276
1978	Gary Player	277
1979	Fuzzy Zoeller	280
1980	Seve Ballesteros	275
1981	Tom Watson	280
1982	Craig Stadler	284
1983	S. Ballesteros	280
1984	Ben Crenshaw	277
1985	Bern. Langer	282
1986	Jack Nicklaus	279
1987	Larry Mize	285

U.S. OPEN CHAMPIONSHIP

YEAR	WINNER	VENUE	SCORE	YEAR	WINNER	VENUE	SCORE
1895	Hor. Rawlins	Newport, RI	173	1940	L. Little	Canterbury, Oh.	287
1896	James Foulis	Shinnecock Hills	152	1941	C. Wood	Colonial, Texas	284
1897	Joe Lloyd	Chicago CC	162	1942–1945 No Championship			
1898	Fred Herd	Myopia CC, Mass	328	1946	L. Mangrum	Canterbury, Oh.	284
1899	Willie Smith	Baltimore, Md	315	1948	L. Worsham	St. Louis, Mo	282
1900	Harry Vardon	Chicago CC	313	1949	C. Middlecoff	Medinah, Ill	286
1901	Wm. Anderson	Myopia CC	331	1950	B.Hogan	Merion GC, Pa	287
1902	L. Auchterlonie	Garden City, NY	307	1951	B.Hogan	Oaklond Hills, Mi	287
1903	Wm. Anderson	Baltrusol CC, NY	307	1952	J. Boros	Northwood, Tex	.281
1904	Wm. Anderson	Glen View, Ill	303	1953	B. Hogan	Oakmont CC, Pa	283
1905	Wm. Anderson	Myopia CC	314	1954	E. Furgol	Baltrusol, NJ	284
1906	Alex Smith	Onwentsia CC, Ill	295	1955	J. Fleck	Olympic CC, Cal	287
1907	Alex Ross	Philadelphia CC	302	1956	C. Middlecoff	Oak Hill, NY	281
1908	Fred McLeod	Myopia CC	322	1957	D. Mayer	Inverness, Ohio	282
1909	George Sargent	Englewood, NY	290	1958	T. Bolt	Southern Hills	283
1910	Alex Smith	Philadelphia CC	298	1959	B. Casper	Winged Foot, NY	282
1911	J. McDermott	Chicago GC	307	1960	A. Palmer	Cherry Hills, Col	280
1912	J. McDermott	Buffalo CC, NY	294	1961	G. Littler	Oakland Hills, Mi	281
1913	Fr. Ouimet (am)	County Club	304	1962	J. Nicklaus	Oakmont, Pa	283
1914	Walter Hagen	Midlothian, Ill	290	1963	J. Boros	Country Club	293
1915	Jerome Travers	Baltrusol, NJ	297	1964	K. Venturi	Congressional	278
1916	Chas Evans Jr	Minikahda, Minn	286	1965	G. Player	Bellerive CC, Mo	282
1917–1918 No Championship				1966	B. Casper	Olympic CC, Cal	278
1919	Walter Hagen	Brae Burn, Mass	301	1967	J. Nicklaus	Baltrusol, NJ	275
1920	Ted Ray	Inverness, Ohio	295	1968	L. Trevino	Oak Hill, NY	275
1921	James Barnes	Columbia, Md.	289	1969	O. Moody	Champions, Tex	281
1922	Gene Sarazen	Skokie CC, Ill	288	1970	A. Jacklin	Hazeltine, Minn	281
1923	R. Jones (am)	Inwood CC, NY	296	1971	L. Trevino	Merion GC, Pa	280
1924	Cyril Walker	Oakland Hills, Mi	297	1972	J. Nicklaus	Pebble Beach	290
1925	W. MacFarlane	Worcester, Mass	291	1973	J. Miller	Oakmont CC, Pa	279
1926	R. Jones (am)	Scioto, Ohio	293	1974	H. Irwin	Winged Foot, NY	287
1927	T. Armour	Oakmont CC, Pa	301	1975	L. Graham	Medinah, Il	287
1928	J. Farrell	Olympia Flds. Ill	294	1976	J. Pate	Atlanta Athletic	277
1929	R. Jones (am)	Winged Foot, NY	294	1977	H. Green	Southern Hills	278
1930	R. Jones (am)	Interlachen, Min	287	1978	A. North	Cherry Hills, Col	285
1931	B. Burke	Inverness, Ohio	292	1979	H. Irwin	Inverness, Ohio	284
1932	G. Sarazen	Fresh Meadows	286	1980	J. Nicklaus	Baltrusol, NJ	272
1933	J. Goodman	North Shore, Ill	287	1981	D. Graham	Merion, Pa	273
1934	Olin Dutra	Merion CC, Pa	293	1982	T. Watson	Pebble Beach	282
1935	S. Parks, Jr.	Oakmont, Pa	299	1983	L. Nelson	Oakmont CC, Pa	280
1936	T. Manero	Baltrusol, NJ	282	1984	F. Zoeller	Winged Foot, NY	276
1937	R. Guldahl	Oakland Hills, Mi	281	1985	A. North	Oakland Hills, Mi	279
1938	R. Guldahl	Cherry Hills, Col.	284	1986	R. Floyd	Shinnecock Hills	279
1939	B. Nelson	Philadelphia CC	284	1987	S. Simpson	San Francisco	277

U.S. PGA CHAMPIONSHIP

YEAR	WINNER & RUNNER-UP	VENUE	SCORE
1916	James Barnes bt. Jock Hutchison	Siwanoy CC, NY	1-hole
1917–1918 No Championship			
1919	James Barnes bt. Fred McLeod	Engineers CC, NY	6 & 5
1920	Jock Hutchison bt. J. D. Edgar	Flossmoor CC, Ill.	1-hole
1921	Walter Hagen bt. James Barnes	Inwood CC, Ny	3 & 2
1922	Gene Sarazen bt. Emmet French	Oakmont CC, Pa.	4 & 3
1923	Gene Sarazen bt. Walter Hagen	Pelham CC, Ny	38th
1924	Walter Hagen bt. James Barnes	Fench Lick CC, Ind	2-holes
1925	Walter Hagen bt. Bill Melhorn	Olympia Fields, Ill	6 & 5
1926	Walter Hagen bt. Leo Digel	Salisbury GC, NY	5 & 3
1927	Walter Hagen bt. Joe Turnesa	Cedar Crest CC, Tex	1-hole
1928	Leo Diegel bt. Al Espinosa	Five Farms CC, Md.	6 & 5
1929	Leo Diegel bt. Johnny Farrell	Hill Crest CC, Cal.	6 & 4
1930	Tommy Armour bt. Gene Sarazen	Fresh Meadow, NY	1-hole
1931	Tom Creavy bt. Denny Shute	Wannamoisett R.I.	2 & 1
1932	Olin Dutra bt. Frank Walsh	Keller CC, Minn	4 & 3
1933	Gene Sarazen bt. Willie Goggin	Blue Mound, Wisc.	5 & 4
1934	Paul Runyan bt. Craig Wood	Park CC, NY	38th
1935	John Revolta bt. Tom Armour	Twin Hills CC, Okl	5 & 4
1936	Denny Shute bt. Jimmy Thomson	Pinehurst CC, NC	3 & 2
1937	Denny Shute bt. Har. McSpaden	Pittsburgh CC, Pa	37th
1938	Paul Runyan bt. Sam Snead	Shawnee CC, Pa	8 & 7
1939	Henry Picard bt. Byron Nelson	Pomonok CC, NY	37th
1940	Byron Nelson bt. Sam Snead	Hershey CC, Pa	1-hole
1941	Vic Ghezzi bt. Byron Nelson	Cherry Hills, Colo	38th
1942	Sam Snead bt. Jim Turnesa	Seaview CC, NJ	2 & 1
1943	No Championship		
1944	Bob Hamilton bt. Byron Nelson	Manito CC, Wash.	1-hole
1945	Byron Nelson bt. Sam Byrd	Morraine CC, Ohio	4 & 3
1946	Ben Hogan bt. Ed Oliver	Portland GC, Ore	6 & 4
1947	Jim Ferrier bt. Chick Harbert	Plum Hollow, Mich.	2 & 1
1948	Ben Hogan bt. Mike Turnesa	Norwood Hills, Mo.	7 & 6
1949	Sam Snead bt. Johnny Palmer	Hermitage CC, Pa	3 & 2
1950	Chandler Harper bt. H. Williams	Scioto CC, Ohio	4 & 3
1951	San Snead bt. Walter Burkemo	Oakmont CC, Pa	7 & 6
1952	Jim Turnesa bt. Chick Harbert	Big Spring CC, Ky.	1-hole
1953	Walter Burkemo bt. Felice Torza	Birmingham, Mich	2 & 1
1954	Chick Harbert bt. Walt. Burkemo	Keller CC, Minn	4 & 3
1955	Doug Ford bt. Cary Middlecoff	Meadowbrook, Mich	4 & 3
1956	Jack Burke bt. Ted Kroll	Blue Hill CC, Mass	3 & 2
1957	Lion Hebert bt. Dow Finsterwald	Miami Valley, Ohio	2 & 1
1958	Dow Finsterwald	Llanerch, Pa	276
1959	Bob Rosburg	Minneapolis CC	277
1960	Jay Hebert	Firestone, Ohio	281
1961	Jerry Barber	Olympia Fields	277
1962	Gary Player	Aronomink, Pa	278
1963	Jack Nicklaus	Dallas AC, Tex	279
1964	Bobby Nichols	Columbus, Ohio	271
1965	Dave Marr	Laurel Valley, Pa	280
1966	Al Gelberger	Firestone, Ohio	280
1967	Don January	Columbine, Colo	281
1968	Julius Boros	Pecan Valley, Tex	281
1969	Ray Floyd	NCR CC, Ohio	276
1970	Dave Stockton	Southern Hills	279
1971	Jack Nicklaus	PGA Natl., Fla	281
1972	Gary Player	Oakland Hills, Mi	281
1973	Jack Nicklaus	Firestone, Ohio	277
1974	Lee Trevino	Tanglewood, NC	276
1975	Jack Nicklaus	Firestone, Ohio	276
1976	Dave Stockton	Congressional	281
1977	Lanny Wadkins	Pebble Beach, Ca	282
1978	John Mahaffey	Oakmont, Pa	276
1979	David Graham	Oakland Hills, Mi	272
1980	Jack Nicklaus	Oak Hill, NY	274
1981	Larry Nelson	Atlanta AC, Ga	273
1982	Ray Floyd	Southern Hills	272
1983	Hal Sutton	Riviera CC, Cal.	274
1984	Lee Trevino	Shoal Creek, Al.	273
1985	Hubert Green	Cherry Hills, Co.	278
1986	Bob Tway	Inverness, Ohio	276
1987	Larry Nelson	West Palm Beach	287

THE RYDER CUP

1927 WORCESTER, MASSACHUSETTS
CAPTAINS TED RAY AND WALTER HAGEN

FOURSOMES:

W. Hagen & J. Golden bt. E. Ray & F. Robson	2 & 1
J. Farrell & J. Turnesa bt. G. Duncan & A. Compston	8 & 6
G. Sarazen & A. Watrous bt. A. G. Havers & H. C. Jolly	3 & 2
L. Diegel & W. Melhorn lost to A. Boomer & C. A. Whitcombe	7 & 5

SINGLES:

Melhorn bt. Compston	1–hole
Farrell bt. Boomer	5 & 4
Golden bt. Jolly	8 & 7
Diegel bt. Ray	7 & 5
Sarazen ½–with Whitcombe	Halved
Hagen bt. Havers	2 & 1
Watrous bt. Robson	3 & 2
Turnesa lost to Duncan	1–hole

RESULT: USA, 9½. BRITAIN, 2½

1929 MOORTOWN, LEEDS
CAPTAINS: TED RAY AND WALTER HAGEN

FOURSOMES:

J. Farrell & J. Turnesa ½–with C. A. Whitcombe & A. Compston	Halved
L. Diegel & A. Espinosa bt. A. Boomer & G. Duncan	7 & 5
G. Sarazen & E. Dudley lost to A. Mitchell & F. Robson	2 & 1
J. Golden & W. Hagen bt. E. R. Whitcombe & H. Cotton	2–holes

SINGLES:

Farrell lost to Whitcombe	8 & 6
Hagen lost to Duncan	10 & 8
Diegel bt. Mitchell	9 & 8
Sarazen lost to Compston	6 & 4
Turnesa lost to Boomer	4 & 3
Smith bt. Robson	4 & 2
Watrous lost to Cotton	4 & 3
Espinosa ½–with Whitcombe	Halved

RESULT: BRITAIN, 7. USA, 5.

1931 SCIOTO, COLUMBUS, OHIO
CAPTAINS: C. A. WHITCOMBE AND WALTER HAGEN

FOURSOMES:

G. Sarazen & J. Farrell bt. A. Compston & W. H. Davies	8 & 7
W. Hagen & D. Shute bt. G. Duncan & A. G. Havers	10 & 9
L. Diegel & A. Espinosa lost to A. Mitchell & F. Robson	3 & 1
W. Burke & W. Cox bt. S. Easterbrook & E. R. Whitcombe	3 & 2

SINGLES

Burke bt. Compston	7 & 6
Sarazen bt. Robson	7 & 6
Farrell lost to Davies	4 & 3
Cox bt. Mitchell	3 & 1
Hagen bt. C. A. Whitcombe	4 & 3
Shute bt. Hodson	8 & 6
Espinosa bt. E. R. Whitcombe	2 & 1
Wood bt. Havers	4 & 3

RESULT: USA, 9. BRITAIN, 3

1933 SOUTHPORT & AINSDALE
CAPTAINS: J. H. TAYLOR AND WALTER HAGEN

FOURSOMES:

Percy Alliss & C. A. Whitcombe ½–with G. Sarazen & W. Hagen	Halved
A. Mitchell & A. G. Havers bt. O. Dutra & D. Shute	3 & 2
W. H. Davies & S. Easterbrook bt. C. Wood & P. Runyan	1–hole
A. H. Padgham & A. Perry lost to E. Dudley & W. Burke	1–hole

SINGLES

Sarazen bt. Padgham	6 & 4
Dutra lost to Mitchell	9 & 8
Hagen bt. Lacey	2 & 1
Wood bt. Davies	4 & 3
Runyan lost to Alliss	2 & 1
Diegel lost to Havers	4 & 3
Shute lost to Easterbrook	1–hole
Smith bt. C. A. Whitcombe	2 & 1

RESULT: BRITAIN, 6½. USA, 5½.

1935 RIDGEWOOD, NEW JERSEY
CAPTAINS: C. A. WHITCOMBE AND WALTER HAGEN

FOURSOMES:

G. Sarazen & W. Hagen bt. A. Perry & J. Busson	7 & 6
H. Picard & J. Revolta bt. A. H. Padgham & Percy Alliss	6 & 5
P. Runyan & H. Smith bt. W. Cox & E. W. Jarman	9 & 8
O. Dutra & K. Laffoon lost to C. A. and E. R. Whitcombe	1–hole

SINGLES:

Sarazen bt. Busson	3 & 2
Runyan bt. Burton	5 & 3
Revolta bt. R. A. Whitcombe	2 & 1
Dutra bt. Padgham	4 & 2
Wood lost to Alliss	1–hole
Smith ½–with Cox	Halved
Picard bt. E. R. Whitcombe	3 & 2
Parks ½–with Perry	Halved

RESULT: USA, 9. BRITAIN, 3

1937 SOUTHPORT & AINSDALE
CAPTAINS: C. A. WHITCOMBE AND WALTER HAGEN

FOURSOMES:

E. Dudley & B. Nelson bt. A. H. Padgham & H. Cotton	4 & 2
R. Guldahl & T. Manero bt. A. Lacey & W. Cox	2 & 1
G. Sarazen & D. Shute ½–with C. A. Whitcombe & D. Rees	Halved
H. Picard & J. Revolta lost to Percy Alliss & R. Burton	2 & 1

SINGLES:

Guldahl bt. Padgham	8 & 7
Shute ½–with King	Halved
Nelson lost to Rees	3 & 1
Manero lost to Cotton	5 & 3
Sarazen bt. Alliss	1–hole
Snead bt. Burton	5 & 4
Dudley bt. Perry	2 & 1
Picard bt. Lacey	2 & 1

RESULT: USA, 8. BRITAIN, 4

1947 PORTLAND, OREGON
CAPTAINS: HENRY COTTON AND BEN HOGAN

FOURSOMES:

E. Oliver & L. Worsham bt. H. Cotton & A. Lees	10 & 9
S. Snead & L. Mangrum bt. F. Daly & C. Ward	6 & 5
B. Hogan & J. Demaret bt. J. Adams & M. Faulkner	2–holes
B. Nelson & H. Barron bt. D. Rees & S. King	2 & 1

SINGLES

Harrison bt. Daly	5 & 4
Worsham bt. Adams	3 & 2
Mangrum bt. Faulkner	6 & 5
Oliver bt. Ward	4 & 3
Nelson bt. Lees	2 & 1
Snead bt. Cotton	5 & 4
Demaret bt. Rees	3 & 2
Keiser lost to King	4 & 3

RESULT: USA, 11. GB & IRE, 1

1949 GANTON
CAPTAINS: C. A. WHITCOMBE AND BEN HOGAN

FOURSOMES:

E. J. Harrison & J. Palmer lost to M. Faulkner & J. Adams	2 & 1
R. Hamilton & S. Alexander lost to F. Daly & K. Bousfield	4 & 2
J. Demaret & C. Heafner bt. C. Ward & S. King	4 & 3
S. Snead & L. Mangrum lost to R. Burton & A. Lees	1–hole

SINGLES:

Harrison bt. Faulkner	8 & 7
J. Palmer lost to Adams	2 & 1
Snead bt. Ward	6 & 5
Hamilton lost to Rees	6 & 4
Heafner bt. Burton	3 & 2
Harbert bt. King	4 & 3
Demaret bt. Lees	7 & 6
Mangrum bt. Daly	4 & 3

RESULT: USA, 7. GB & IRE, 5

1951 PINEHURST, NORTH CAROLINA
CAPTAINS: A. J. LACEY AND SAM SNEAD

FOURSOMES:

C. Heafner & J. Burke bt. M. Faulkner & D. Rees	5 & 3
E. Oliver & H. Ransom lost to C. Ward & A. Lees	2 & 1
S. Snead & L. Mangrum bt. J. Adams & J. Panton	5 & 4
B. Hogan & J. Demaret bt. F. Daly & K. Bousfield	5 & 4

SINGLES:

Burke bt. Adams	4 & 3
Demaret bt. Rees	2–holes
Heafner ½–with Daly	Halved
Mangrum bt. Weetman	6 & 5
Oliver lost to Lees	2 & 1
Hogan bt. Ward	3 & 2
Alexander bt. Panton	8 & 7
Snead bt. Faulkner	4 & 3

RESULT: USA, 9½. GB & IRE, 2½

1953 WENTWORTH
CAPTAINS: HENRY COTTON AND LLOYD MANGRUM

FOURSOMES:

D. Douglas & E. Oliver bt. H. Weetman & P. Alliss	2 & 1
L. Mangrum & S. Snead bt. E. Brown & J. Panton	8 & 7
T. Kroll & J. Burke bt. J. Adams & B. J. Hunt	7 & 5
W. Burkemo & C. Middlecoff lost to F. Daly & H. Bradshaw	1–hole

SINGLES:

Burke bt. Rees	2 & 1
Kroll lost to Daly	9 & 7
Mangrum lost to Brown	2–holes
Snead lost to Weetman	1–hole
Middlecoff bt. Faulkner	3 & 1
Turnesa bt. Alliss	1–hole
Douglas ½–with Hunt	Halved
Haas lost to Bradshaw	3 & 2

RESULT: USA, 6½. GB & IRE, 5½

1955 THUNDERBIRD GOLF & CC, CALIFORNIA
CAPTAINS: DAI REES AND CHICK HARBERT

FOURSOMES:

C. Harper & J. Barber lost to J. Fallon & J. Jacobs	1–hole
D. Ford & T. Kroll bt. E. Brown & S. Scott	5 & 4
J. Burke & T. Bolt bt. A. Lees & H. Weetman	1–hole
S. Snead & C. Middlecoff bt. H. Bradshaw & D. Rees	3 & 2

SINGLES:

Bolt bt. O'Connor	4 & 2
Harbert bt. Scott	3 & 2
Middlecoff lost to Jacobs	1–hole
Snead bt. Rees	3 & 1
Furgol lost to Lees	3 & 2
Barber lost to Brown	3 & 2
Burke bt. Bradshaw	3 & 2
Ford bt. Weetman	3 & 2

RESULT: USA, 8. GB & IRE, 4.

1957 LINDRICK, SHEFFIELD
CAPTAINS: DAI REES AND JACK BURKE

FOURSOMES:

P. Alliss & B. J. Hunt lost to D. Ford & D. Finsterwald	2 & 1
K. Bousfield & D. Rees bt. A. Wall & F. Hawkins	3 & 2
M. Faulkner & H. Weetman lost to T. Kroll & J. Burke	4 & 3
C. O'Connor & E. Brown lost to R. Mayer & T. Bolt	7 & 5

SINGLES:

Brown bt. Bolt	4 & 3
Mills bt. Burke	5 & 3
Alliss lost to Hawkins	2 & 1
Bousfield bt. Hebert	4 & 3
Rees bt. Furgol	7 & 6
Hunt bt. Ford	6 & 5
O'Connor bt. Finsterwald	7 & 6
Bradshaw ½–with Mayer	Halved

RESULT: GB & IRE, 7½. USA, 4½

THE RYDER CUP

1959 ELDORADO CC, CALIFORNIA
CAPTAINS: DAI REES AND SAM SNEAD

FOURSOMES:

R. Rosburg & M. Souchak bt. B. J. Hunt & E. Brown	5 & 4
J. Boros & J. Finsterwald bt. D. Rees & K. Bousfield	2–holes
A. Wall & D. Ford lost to C. O'Connor & P. Alliss	3 & 2
S. Snead & C. Middlecoff ½–with H. Weetman & D. Thomas	Halved

SINGLES:

Ford ½–with Drew	Halved
Souchak bt. Bousfield	3 & 2
Rosburg bt. Weetman	6 & 5
Snead bt. Thomas	6 & 5
Wall bt. O'Connor	7 & 6
Finsterwald bt. Rees	1–hole
Hebert ½–with Alliss	Halved
Middlecoff lost to Brown	4 & 3

RESULT: USA, 8½. GB & IRE, 3½

1961 ROYAL LYTHAM & ST. ANNES
CAPTAINS: DAI REES AND JERRY BARBER

FOURSOMES:

D. Ford & G. Littler lost to C. O'Connor & P. Allis	4 & 3
A. Wall & J. Hebert bt. J. Panton & B. J. Hunt	4 & 3
W. Casper & A. Palmer bt. D. Rees & K. Bousfield	2 & 1
W. Collins & M. Souchak bt. T. Haliburton & N. Coles	1–hole

FOURSOMES (2):

A. Wall & J. Hebert bt. C. O'Connor & P. Alliss	1–hole
W. Casper & A. Palmer bt. J. Panton & B. Hunt	5 & 4
W. Collins & M. Souchak lost to D. Rees & K. Bousfield	4 & 2
J. Barber & D. Finsterwald bt. T. Haliburton & N. Coles	1–hole

SINGLES (1):

D. Ford bt. H. Weetman	1–hole
M. Souchak bt. R. Moffitt	5 & 4
A. Palmer ½–with P. Alliss	Halved
W. Casper bt. K. Bousfield	5 & 3
J. Hebert lost to D. Rees	2 & 1
G. Littler ½–with N. Coles	Halved
J. Barber lost to B. Hunt	5 & 4
D. Finsterwald bt. C. O'Connor	2 & 1

SINGLES (2):

A. Wall bt. H. Weetman	1–hole
W. Collins lost to P. Alliss	3 & 2
M. Souchak bt. B. Hunt	2 & 1
A. Palmer bt. T. Haliburton	2 & 1
D. Ford lost to D. Rees	4 & 3
J. Barber lost to K. Bousfield	1–hole
D. Finsterwald lost to N. Coles	1–hole
G. Littler ½–with C. O'Connor	Halved

RESULT: USA, 14½. GB & IRE, 9½

1963 ATLANTA, GEORGIA
CAPTAINS: JOHNNY FALLON AND ARNOLD PALMER

FOURSOMES (1):

A. Palmer & J. Pott lost to B. Huggett & G. Will	3 & 2
W. Casper & D. Ragan bt. C. O'Connor & P. Alliss	1–hole
J. Boros & A. Lema ½–with N. Coles & B. Hunt	Halved
G. Littler & D. Finsterwald ½–with D. Thomas & H. Weetman	Halved

FOURSOMES (2):

W. Maxwell & R. Goalby bt. D. Thomas & H. Weetman	4 & 3
A. Palmer & W. Casper bt. B. Huggett & G. Will	5 & 4
G. Littler & D. Finsterwald bt. N. Coles & G. M. Hunt	2 & 1
J. Boros & A. Lema bt. T. Haliburton B. Hunt	1–hole

FOURBALLS (1):

A. Palmer & D. Finsterwald bt. B. Huggett & D. Thomas	5 & 4
G. Littler & J. Boros ½–with P. Alliss & B. Hunt	Halved
W. Casper & W. Maxwell bt. H. Weetman & G. Will	3 & 2
R. Goalby & D. Ragan lost to N. Coles & C. O'Connor	1–hole

FOURBALLS (2):

A. Palmer & D. Finsterwald bt. N. Coles & C. O'Connor	3 & 2
A. Lema & J. Pott bt. P. Alliss & B. Hunt	1–hole
W. Casper & W. Maxwell bt. T. Haliburton & G. M. Hunt	2 & 1
R. Goalby & D. Ragan ½–with B. Huggett & D. Thomas	Halved

SINGLES (1):

Lema bt. Hunt	5 & 3

Pott lost to Huggett	3 & 1
Palmer lost to Alliss	1–hole
Casper ½–with Coles	Halved
Goalby bt. Thomas	3 & 2
Littler bt. O'Connor	1–hole
Boros lost to Weetman	1–hole
Finsterwald lost to B. Hunt	2–holes

SINGLES (2):

Palmer bt. Will	3 & 2
Ragan bt. Coles	2 & 1
Lema ½–with Alliss	Halved
Littler bt. Haliburton	6 & 5
Boros bt. Weetman	2 & 1
Maxwell bt. O'Connor	2 & 1
Finsterwald bt. Thomas	4 & 3
Goalby bt. B. Hunt	2 & 1

RESULT: USA, 23. GB & IRE, 9

1965 ROYAL BIRKDALE
CAPTAINS: HARRY WEETMAN AND BYRON NELSON

FOURSOMES (1):

J. Boros & A. Lema bt. L. Platts & P. Butler	1–hole
A. Palmer & D. Marr lost to D. Thomas & G. Will	6 & 5
W. Casper & G. Littler bt. B. Hunt & N. Coles	2 & 1
K. Venturi & D. January lost to P. Alliss & C. O'Connor	5 & 4

FOURSOMES (2):

A. Palmer & D. Marr bt. D. Thomas & G. Will	6 & 5
W. Casper & G. Littler lost to P. Alliss & C. O'Connor	2 & 1
J. Boros & A. Lema lost to J. Martin & J. Hitchcock	5 & 4
K. Venturi & D. January lost to B. Hunt & N. Coles	3 & 2

FOURBALLS (1):

D. January & T. Jacobs bt. D. Thomas & G. Will	1–hole
W. Casper & G. Littler ½–with L. Platts & P. Butler	Halved
A. Palmer & D. Marr bt. P. Alliss & C. O'Connor	6 & 4
J. Boros & A. Lema lost to B. Hunt & N. Coles	1–hole

FOURBALLS (2):

A. Palmer & D. Marr lost to P. Alliss & C. O'Connor	2–holes
D. January & T. Jacobs bt. D. Thomas & G. Will	1–hole
W. Casper & G. Littler ½–with L. Platts & P. Butler	Halved
K. Venturi & A. Lema bt. B. Hunt & N. Coles	1–hole

SINGLES (1):

Palmer bt. Hitchcock	3 & 2
Boros bt. Platts	4 & 2
Lema bt. Butler	1–hole
Marr bt. Coles	2–holes
Littler lost to B. Hunt	2–holes
T. Jacobs bt. Thomas	2 & 1
Casper lost to Alliss	1–hole
January ½–with Will	Halved

SINGLES (2):

Lema bt. O'Connor	6 & 4
Boros bt. Hitchcock	2 & 1
Palmer bt. Butler	2–holes
Venturi lost to Alliss	3 & 1
Casper lost to Coles	3 & 2
Littler bt. Will	2 & 1
Marr bt. B. Hunt	1–hole
T. Jacobs lost to Platts	1–hole

RESULT: USA, 19½. GB & IRE, 12½

1967 HOUSTON, TEXAS
CAPTAINS: DAI REES AND BEN HOGAN

FOURSOMES (1):

W. Casper & J. Boros ½–with B. Huggett & C. Will	Halved
A. Palmer & G. Dickinson bt. P. Alliss & C. O'Connor	2 & 1
D. Sanders & G. Brewer lost to A. Jacklin & N. Coles	4 & 3
R. Nichols & J. Pott bt. B. Hunt & N. Coles	6 & 5

FOURSOMES (2):

W. Casper & J. Boros bt. B. Huggett & G. Will	1–hole
G. Dickinson & A. Palmer bt. M. Gregson & H. Boyle	5 & 4
G. Littler & A. Geiberger lost to A. Jacklin & D. Thomas	3 & 2
R. Nichols & J. Pott bt. P. Alliss & C. O'Connor	2 & 1

FOURBALLS (1):

W. Casper & G. Brewer bt. P. Alliss & C. O'Connor	3 & 2

R. Nichols & J. Pott bt. B. Hunt & N. Coles	1–hole
G. Littler & A. Geiberger bt. A. Jacklin & D. Thomas	1–hole
G. Dickinson & D. Sanders bt. B. Huggett & G. Will	3 & 2

FOURBALLS (2):

W. Casper & G. Brewer bt. B. Hunt & N. Coles	5 & 3
G. Dickinson & D. Sanders bt. P. Alliss & M. Gregson	3 & 2
A. Palmer & J. Boros bt. G. Will & H. Boyle	1–hole
G. Littler & A. Geiberger ½–with A. Jacklin & D. Thomas	Halved

SINGLES (1):

Brewer bt. Boyle	4 & 3
Casper bt. Alliss	2 & 1
Palmer bt. Jacklin	3 & 2
Boros lost to Huggett	1–hole
Sanders lost to Coles	2 & 1
Geiberger bt. Gregson	4 & 2
Littler ½–with Thomas	Halved
Nichols ½–with B. Hunt	Halved

SINGLES (2):

Palmer bt. Huggett	5 & 3
Brewer lost to Alliss	2 & 1
Dickinson bt. Jacklin	3 & 2
Pott bt. Will	3 & 1
Geiberger bt. Gregson	2 & 1
Boros ½–with B. Hunt	Halved
Sanders lost to Coles	2 & 1

RESULT: USA, 23½. GB & IRE, 8½

1969 ROYAL BIRKDALE
CAPTAINS: ERIC BROWN AND SAM SNEAD

FOURSOMES (1):

N. Coles & B. Huggett bt. M. Barber & R. Floyd	3 & 2
B. Gallagher & M. Bembridge bt. L. Trevino & K. Still	2 & 1
A. Jacklin & P. Townsend bt. D. Hill & T. Aaron	3 & 1
C. O'Connor & P. Alliss ½–with W. Casper & F. Beard	Halved

FOURSOMES (2):

N. Coles & B. Huggett lost to D. Hill & T. Aaron	1–hole
B. Gallacher & M. Bembridge lost to L. Trevino & G. Littler	1–hole
A. Jacklin & P. Townsend lost to W. Casper & F. Beard	1–hole
P. Butler & B. Hunt lost to J. Nicklaus & D. Sikes	1–hole

FOURBALLS (1):

C. O'Connor & P. Townsend bt. D. Hill & D. Douglass	1–hole
B. Huggett & A. Caygill ½–with R. Floyd & M. Barber	Halved
B. Barnes & P. Alliss lost to L. Trevino & G. Littler	1–hole
A. Jacklin & N. Coles bt. J. Nicklaus & D. Sikes	1–hole

FOURBALLS (2):

P. Butler & P. Townsend lost to W. Casper & F. Beard	2–holes
B. Huggett & B. Gallacher lost to D. Hill & K. Still	2 & 1
M. Bembridge & P. Hunt ½–with T. Aaron & R. Floyd	Halved
A. Jacklin & N. Coles ½–with L. Trevino & M. Barber	Halved

SINGLES (1):

Alliss lost to Trevino	2 & 1
Townsend lost to Hill	5 & 4
Coles bt. Aaron	1–hole
Barnes lost to Casper	1–hole
O'Connor bt. Beard	5 & 4
Bembridge bt. Still	1–hole
Butler bt. Floyd	1–hole
Jacklin bt. Nicklaus	4 & 3

SINGLES (2):

Barnes lost to Hill	4 & 2
Gallacher bt. Trevino	4 & 3
Bembridge lost to Barber	7 & 6
Butler bt. Douglass	3 & 2
Coles lost to Sikes	4 & 3
O'Connor lost to Littler	2 & 1
Huggett ½–with Casper	Halved
Jacklin ½–with Nicklaus	Halved

RESULT: GB & IRE, 16. USA, 16

THE RYDER CUP

1971 ST. LOUIS, MISSOURI

CAPTAINS: ERIC BROWN AND JAY HEBERT

FOURSOMES (1):

W. Casper & M. Barber lost to N. Coles & C. O'Connor	2 & 1
A. Palmer & G. Dickinson bt. P. Townsend & P. Oosterhuis	2–holes
J. Nicklaus & D. Stockton lost to B. Huggett & A. Jacklin	3 & 2
C. Coody & F. Beard lost to M. Bembridge & P. Butler	1–hole

FOURSOMES (2):

W. Casper & M. Barber lost to H. Bannerman & B. Gallacher	2 & 1
A. Palmer & G. Dickinson bt. P. Townsend & P. Oosterhuis	1–hole
L. Trevino & M. Rudolph ½–with B. Huggett & A. Jacklin	Halved
J. Nicklaus & J. C. Snead bt. M. Bembridge & P. Butler	5 & 3

FOURBALLS (1):

L. Trevino & M. Rudolph bt. C. O'Connor & B. Barnes	2 & 1
F. Beard & J. C. Snead bt. N. Coles & J. Garner	2 & 1
A. Palmer & G. Dickinson bt. P. Oosterhuis & B. Gallacher	5 & 4
J. Nicklaus & G. Littler bt. P. Townsend & H. Bannerman	2 & 1

FOURBALLS (2):

L. Trevino & W. Casper lost to B. Gallacher & P. Oosterhuis	1–hole
G. Littler & J. C. Snead bt. A. Jacklin & B. Huggett	2 & 1
A. Palmer & J. Nicklaus bt. P. Townsend & H. Bannerman	1–hole
C. Coody & F. Beard ½–with N. Coles & C. O'Connor	Halved

SINGLES (1):

Trevino bt. Jacklin	1–hole
Stockton ½–with Gallacher	Halved
Rudolph lost to Barnes	1–hole
Littler lost to Oosterhuis	4 & 3
Nicklaus bt. Townsend	3 & 2
Dickinson bt. O'Connor	5 & 4
Palmer ½–with Bannerman	Halved
Beard ½–with Coles	Halved

SINGLES (2):

Trevino bt. Huggett	7 & 6
Snead bt. Jacklin	1–hole
Barber lost to Barnes	2 & 1
Stockton bt. Townsend	1–hole
Coody lost to Gallacher	2 & 1
Nicklaus bt. Coles	5 & 3
Palmer lost to Oosterhuis	3 & 2
Dickinson lost to Bannerman	2 & 1

RESULT: USA, 18½. GB & IRE, 13½

1973 MUIRFIELD, SCOTLAND

CAPTAINS: BERNARD HUNT AND JACK BURKE

FOURSOMES (1):

L. Trevino & B. Casper lost to B. Barnes & B. Gallacher	1–hole
T. Weiskopf & J. C. Snead lost to C. O'Connor & N. Coles	3 & 2
J. Rodriguez & L. Graham ½–with A. Jacklin & P. Oosterhuis	Halved
J. Nicklaus & A. Palmer bt. M. Bembridge & E. Polland	6 & 5

FOURBALLS (1):

T. Aaron & G. Brewer lost to B. Barnes & B. Gallacher	5 & 4
A. Palmer & J. Nicklaus lost to M. Bembridge & B. Huggett	3 & 1
T. Weiskopf & B. Casper lost to A. Jacklin & P. Oosterhuis	3 & 1
L. Trevino & H. Blancas bt. C O'Connor & N. Coles	2 & 1

FOURSOMES (2):

J. Nicklaus & T. Weiskopf bt. B. Barnes & P. Butler	1–hole
A. Palmer & D. Hill lost to P. Oosterhuis & A. Jacklin	2–holes
J. Rodriguez & L. Graham lost to M. Bembridge & B. Huggett	5 & 4
L. Trevino & B. Casper bt. N. Coles & C. O'Connor	2 & 1

FOURBALLS (2):

J. C. Snead & A. Palmer bt. B. Barnes & P. Butler	2–holes
G. Brewer & B. Casper bt. A. Jacklin & P. Oosterhuis	3 & 2
J. Nicklaus & T. Weiskopf bt. C. Clark & E. Polland	3 & 2
L. Trevino & H. Blancas ½–with M. Bembridge & B. Huggett	Halved

SINGLES (1):

Casper bt. Barnes	2 & 1
Weiskopf bt. Gallacher	3 & 1
Blancas bt. Butler	5 & 4
Aaron lost to Jacklin	3 & 1
Brewer ½–with Coles	Halved
Snead bt. O'Connor	1–hole
Nicklaus ½–with Bembridge	Halved
Trevino ½–with Oosterhuis	Halved

SINGLES (2):

Blancas lost to Huggett	4 & 2
Snead bt. Barnes	3 & 1
Brewer bt. Gallacher	6 & 5
Casper bt. Jacklin	2 & 1
Trevino bt. Coles	6 & 5
Weiskopf ½–with O'Connor	Halved
Nicklaus bt. Bembridge	2–holes
Palmer lost to Oosterhuis	4 & 2

RESULT: USA, 19. GB & IRE, 13

1975 LAUREL VALLEY, PENNSYLVANIA

CAPTAINS: BERNARD HUNT AND ARNOLD PALMER

FOURSOMES (1):

J. Nicklaus & T. Weiskopf bt. B. Barnes & B. Gallacher	5 & 4
G. Littler & H. Irwin bt. N. Wood & M. Bembridge	4 & 3
A. Geiberger & J. Miller bt. A. Jacklin & P. Oosterhuis	3 & 1
L. Trevino & J. C. Snead bt. T. Horton & J. O'Leary	2 & 1

FOURBALLS (1):

B. Casper & R. Floyd lost to A. Jacklin & P. Oosterhuis	2 & 1
T. Weiskopf & L. Graham bt. E. Darcy & C. O'Connor Jnr	3 & 2
J. Nicklaus & B. Murphy ½–with B. Barnes & B. Gallacher	Halved
L. Trevino & H. Irwin bt. T. Horton & J. O'Leary	2 & 1

FOURBALLS (2):

B. Casper & J. Miller ½–with A. Jacklin & P. Oosterhuis	Halved
J. Nicklaus & J. C. Snead bt. T. Horton & N. Wood	4 & 2
G. Littler & L. Graham bt. B. Barnes & B. Gallacher	5 & 3
A. Geiberger & R. Floyd ½–with E. Darcy & G. Hunt	Halved

FOURSOMES (2):

L. Trevino & B. Murphy lost to A. Jacklin & B. Barnes	3 & 2
T. Weiskopf & J. Miller bt. C. O'Connor Jnr & J. O'Leary	5 & 3
H. Irwin & B. Casper bt. P. Oosterhuis & M. Bembridge	3 & 2
A. Geiberger & L. Graham bt. E. Darcy & G. Hunt	3 & 2

SINGLES (1):

Murphy bt. Jacklin	2 & 1
Miller lost to Oosterhuis	2–holes
Trevino ½–with Gallacher	Halved
Irwin ½–with Horton	Halved
Littler bt. Huggett	4 & 2
Casper bt. Darcy	3 & 2
Weiskopf bt. G. Hunt	5 & 3
Nicklaus lost to Barnes	4 & 2

SINGLES (2):

Floyd bt. Jacklin	1–hole
Snead lost to Oosterhuis	3 & 2
Geiberger ½–with Gallacher	Halved
Graham lost to Horton	2 & 1
Irwin bt. O'Leary	2 & 1
Murphy bt. Bembridge	2 & 1
Trevino lost to Wood	2 & 1
Nicklaus lost to Barnes	2 & 1

RESULT: USA, 21. GB & IRE, 11

THE RYDER CUP

1977 ROYAL LYTHAM & ST. ANNES
CAPTAINS: BRIAN HUGGETT AND DOW FINSTERWALD

FOURSOMES:

L. Wadkins & H. Irwin bt. B. Gallacher & B. Barnes	3 & 1
D. Stockton & J. McGee bt. N. Coles & P. Dawson	1—hole
R. Floyd & L. Graham lost to N. Faldo & P. Oosterhuis	2 & 1
E. Sneed & D. January ½—with E. Darcy & A. Jacklin	Halved
J. Nicklaus & T. Watson bt. T. Horton & M. James	5 & 4

FOURBALLS:

T. Watson & H. Green bt. B. Barnes & T. Horton	5 & 4
E. Sneed & L. Wadkins bt. N. Coles & P. Dawson	5 & 3
J. Nicklaus & R. Floyd lost to N. Faldo & P. Oosterhuis	3 & 1
D. Hill & D. Stockton bt. A. Jacklin & E. Darcy	5 & 3
H. Irwin & L. Graham bt. M. James & K. Brown	1—hole

SINGLES:

Wadkins bt. Clark	4 & 3
Graham bt. Coles	5 & 3
January lost to Dawson	5 & 4
Irwin lost to Barnes	1—hole
Hill bt. Horton	5 & 4
Nicklaus lost to Gallacher	1—hole
Green bt. Darcy	1—hole
Floyd bt. James	2 & 1
Watson lost to Faldo	1—hole
McGee bt. Oosterhuis	2—holes

RESULT: USA, 12½. GB & IRE, 7½

1979 GREENBRIER, WEST VIRGINIA
CAPTAINS: JOHN JACOBS AND BILLY CASPER

FOURBALLS (1):

L. Wadkins & L. Nelson bt. A. Garrido & S. Ballesteros	2 & 1
F. Zoeller & L. Trevino bt. K. Brown & M. James	3 & 2
A. Bean & L. Elder bt. P. Oosterhuis & N. Faldo	2 & 1
H. Irwin & J. Mahaffey lost to B. Gallacher & B. Barnes	2 & 1

FOURSOMES (1):

H. Irwin & T. Kite bt. K. Brown & D. Smyth	7 & 6
F. Zoeller & H. Green lost to S. Ballesteros & A. Garrido	3 & 2
L. Trevino & G. Morgan ½—with A. Lyle & A. Jacklin	Halved
L. Wadkins & L. Nelson bt. B. Gallacher & B. Barnes	4 & 3

FOURSOMES (2):

L. Elder & J. Mahaffey lost to A. Jacklin & S. Lyle	5 & 4
A. Bean & T. Kite lost to N. Faldo & P. Oosterhuis	6 & 5
F. Zoeller & M. Hayes lost to B. Gallacher & B. Barnes	2 & 1
L. Wadkins & L. Nelson bt. S. Ballesteros & A. Garrido	3 & 2

FOURBALLS (2):

L. Wadkins & L. Nelson bt. S. Ballesteros & A. Garrido	5 & 4
H. Irwin & T. Kite bt. A. Jacklin & S. Lyle	1—hole
L. Trevino & F. Zoeller lost to B. Gallacher & B. Barnes	3 & 2
L. Elder & M. Hayes lost to N. Faldo & P. Oosterhuis	1—hole

SINGLES:

Wadkins lost to Gallacher	3 & 2
Nelson bt. Ballesteros	3 & 2
Kite bt. Jacklin	1—hole
Hayes bt. Garrido	1—hole
Bean bt. King	4 & 3
Mahaffey bt. Barnes	1—hole
Elder lost to Faldo	3 & 2
Irwin bt. Smyth	5 & 3
Green bt. Oosterhuis	2—holes
Zoeller lost to Brown	1—hole
Trevino bt. Lyle	2 & 1
G. Morgan halved match with M. James	

RESULT: USA, 17. EUR, 11

1981 WALTON HEATH
CAPTAINS: JOHN JACOBS AND DAVE MARR

FOURSOMES (1):

L. Trevino & L. Nelson bt. B. Langer & M. Pinero	1—hole
B. Rogers & B. Leitzke lost to S. Lyle & M. James	2 & 1
H. Irwin & R. Floyd lost to B. Gallacher & D. Smyth	3 & 2
T. Watson & J. Nicklaus bt. P. Oosterhuis & N. Faldo	4 & 3

FOURBALLS (1):

T. Kite & J. Miller ½—with S. Torrance & H. Clark	Halved
B. Crenshaw & J. Pate lost to S. Lyle & M. James	3 & 2
B. Rogers & B. Leitzke lost to D. Smith & J. M. Canizares	6 & 5
H. Irwin & R. Floyd bt. B. Gallacher & E. Darcy	2 & 1

FOURSOMES (2):

L. Trevino & J. Pate bt. P. Oosterhuis & S. Torrance	2 & 1
J. Nicklaus & T. Watson bt. S. Lyle & M. James	3 & 2
B. Rogers & R. Floyd bt. B. Langer & M. Pinero	3 & 2
T. Kite & L. Nelson bt. D. Smyth & B. Gallacher	3 & 2

FOURBALLS (2):

L. Trevino & J. Pate bt. N. Faldo & S. Torrance	7 & 5
L. Nelson & T. Kite bt. S. Lyle & M. James	1—hole
R. Floyd & H. Irwin lost to B. Langer & M. Pinero	2 & 1
J. Nicklaus & T. Watson bt. J. M. Canizares & D. Smyth	3 & 2

SINGLES:

Trevino bt. Torrance	5 & 3
Kite bt. Lyle	3 & 2
Rogers ½—with Gallacher	Halved
Nelson bt. James	2—holes
Crenshaw bt. Smyth	6 & 4
Lietzke ½—with Langer	Halved
Pate lost to Pinero	4 & 2
Irwin bt. Canizares	1—hole
Miller lost to Faldo	2 & 1
Watson lost to Clark	4 & 3
Floyd bt. Oosterhuis	1—hole
Nicklaus bt. Darcy	5 & 3

RESULT: USA, 18½. EUR, 9½

1983 PGA NATIONAL, PALM BEACH GARDENS, FLORIDA
CAPTAINS: TONY JACKLIN AND JACK NICKLAUS

FOURSOMES (1):

T. Watson & B. Crenshaw bt. B. Gallacher & S. Lyle	5 & 4
L. Wadkins & C. Stadler lost to N. Faldo & B. Langer	4 & 2
T. Kite & C. Peete bt. S. Ballesteros & P. Way	2 & 1
R. Floyd & R. Gilder lost to J. M. Canizares & S. Torrance	4 & 3

FOURBALLS (1):

G. Morgan & F. Zoeller lost to B. Waites & K. Brown	2 & 1
T. Watson & J. Haas bt. N. Faldo & B. Langer	2 & 1
R. Floyd & C. Strange lost to S. Ballesteros & P. Way	1—hole
B. Crenshaw & C. Peete ½—with S. Torrance & I. Woosnam	Halved

FOURSOMES (2):

T. Kite & R. Floyd lost to N. Faldo & B. Langer	3 & 2
J. Haas & C. Strange bt. B. Waites & K. Brown	3 & 2
G. Morgan & L. Wadkins bt. S. Torrance & J. M. Canizares	7 & 5
T. Watson & B. Gilder lost to S. Ballesteros & P. Way	2 & 1

FOURBALLS (2):

L. Wadkins & C. Stadler bt. B. Waites & K. Brown	1—hole
B. Crenshaw & C. Peete lost to N. Faldo & B. Langer	4 & 2
G. Morgan & J. Haas ½—with S. Ballesteros & P. Way	Halved
T. Watson & B. Gilder bt. S. Torrance & I. Woosnam	5 & 4

SINGLES:

Zoeller ½—with Ballesteros	Halved
Haas lost to Faldo	2 & 1
Morgan lost to Langer	2—holes
Gilder bt. Brand	2—holes
Crenshaw bt. Lyle	3 & 1
Peete bt. Waites	1—hole
Strange lost to Way	2 & 1
Kite ½—with Torrance	Halved
Stadler bt. Woosnam	3 & 2
Wadkins ½—with Canizares	Halved
Floyd lost to Brown	4 & 3
Watson bt. Gallacher	2 & 1

RESULT: USA, 14½. EUR, 13½

1985 THE BELFRY, SUTTON COLDFIELD
CAPTAINS: TONY JACKLIN AND LEE TREVINO

FOURSOMES (1):

S. Ballesteros & M. Pinero bt. C. Strange & M. O'Meara	2 & 1
B. Langer & N. Faldo lost to C. Peete & T. Kite	3 & 2
S. Lyle & K. Brown lost to L. Wadkins & R. Floyd	4 & 3
H. Clark & S. Torrance lost to C. Stadler & H. Sutton	3 & 2

FOURBALLS (1):

P. Way & I. Woosnam bt. F. Zoeller & H. Green	1—hole
S. Ballesteros & M. Pinero bt. A. North & P. Jacobsen	2 & 1
B. Langer & J. M. Canizares ½—with C. Stadler & H. Sutton	Halved
S. Torrance & H. Clark lost to R. Floyd & L. Wadkins	1—hole

FOURBALLS (2):

S. Torrance & H. Clark bt. T. Kite & A. North	2 & 1
P. Way & I. Woosnam bt. H. Green & F. Zoeller	4 & 3
S. Ballesteros & M. Pinero lost to M. O'Meara & L. Wadkins	3 & 2
B. Langer & S. Lyle ½—with C. Stadler & C. Strange	Halved

FOURSOMES (2):

J. M. Canizares & J. Rivero bt. T. Kite & C. Peete	7 & 5
S. Ballesteros & M. Pinero bt. C. Stadler & H. Sutton	5 & 4
P. Way & I. Woosnam lost to C. Strange & P. Jacobsen	4 & 2
B. Langer & K. Brown bt. R. Floyd & L. Wadkins	3 & 2

SINGLES:

Pinero bt. Wadkins	3 & 1
Woosnam lost to Stadler	2 & 1
Way bt. Floyd	2—holes
Ballesteros ½—with Kite	Halved
Lyle bt. Jacobsen	3 & 2
Langer bt. Sutton	5 & 4
Torrance bt. North	1—hole
Clark bt. O'Meara	1—hole
Rivero lost to Peete	1—hole
Faldo lost to Green	3 & 1
Canizares bt. Zoeller	2—holes
Brown lost to Strange	4 & 2

RESULT: EUR, 16½. USA, 11½

1987 MUIRFIELD VILLAGE, OHIO
CAPTAINS: TONY JACKLIN AND JACK NICKLAUS

FOURSOMES (1):

Torrance & Clark lost to Strange & Kite	4 & 2
Brown & Langer lost to Sutton & Pohl	2 & 1
Faldo & Woosnam bt. Wadkins & Mize	2—holes
Ballesteros & Olazabal bt. Nelson & Stewart	1—hole

FOURBALLS (1):

Brand Jr. & Rivero bt. Crenshaw & Simpson	3 & 2
Lyle & Langer bt. Bean & Calcavecchia	1—hole
Faldo & Woosnam bt. Sutton & Pohl	2 & 1
Ballesteros & Olazabal bt. Strange & Kite	2 & 1

FOURSOMES (2):

Rivero & Brand lost to Strange & Kite	3 & 1
Faldo & Woosnam ½—with Sutton & Mize	Halved
Lyle & Langer bt. Wadkins & Nelson	2 & 1
Ballesteros & Olazabal bt. Crenshaw & Stewart	1—hole

FOURBALLS (2):

Woosnam & Faldo bt. Kite & Strange	5 & 4
Darcy & Brand lost to Bean & Stewart	3 & 2
Ballesteros & Olazabal lost to Sutton & Mize	2 & 1
Lyle & Langer bt. Wadkins & Nelson	1—hole

SINGLES:

I. Woosnam lost to A. Bean	1—hole
H. Clark bt. D. Pohl	1—hole
S. Torrance ½—with L. Mize	Halved
N. Faldo lost to M. Calcavecchia	1—hole
J.-M. Olazabal lost to P. Stewart	2—holes
J. Rivero lost to S. Simpson	2 & 1
S. Lyle lost to T. Kite	3 & 2
E. Darcy bt. B. Crenshaw	1—hole
B. Langer ½—with L. Nelson	Halved
S. Ballesteros bt. C. Strange	2 & 1
K. Brown lost to L. Wadkins	3 & 2
G. Brand Jr. ½—with H. Sutton	Halved

RESULT: EUR, 15. USA, 13.

WALKER CUP RESULTS

1922 NATIONAL GOLF LINKS OF AMERICA, N.Y.

CAPTAINS: R. HARRIS AND W.C. FOWNES JR.

FOURSOMES:

C. Tolley & B. Darwin lost to J. Guilford & F. Quimet	8 & 7
R. Wethered & C. Aylmer bt. C. Evans Jr. & R. Gardner	5 & 4
W. Torrance & C. Hooman lost to R. Jones Jr. & J. Sweetser	3 & 2
J. Caven & W. Mackenzie lost to M. Marston & W. Fownes Jr.	2 & 1

SINGLES:

C. Tolley lost to J. Guilford	2 & 1
R. Wethered lost to Jones	3 & 2
Caven lost to Evans Jr.	5 & 4
Alymer lost to Ouimet	8 & 7
Torrance lost to Gardner	7 & 5
Mackenzie bt. Marston	6 & 5
Darwin bt. Fownes Jr.	6 & 5
C. Hooman bt. Sweetser	37th

RESULTS: USA, 8. GB & IRE, 4.

1923 ST. ANDREWS

CAPTAINS: CYRIL TOLLEY AND ROBERT GARDINER

FOURSOMES:

C. Tolley & R. Wethered bt. F. Ouimet & J. Sweetser	6 & 5
R. Harris & C. Hooman lost to R. Gardiner & M. Marston	7 & 6
E. Holderness & W. Hope bt. G. Rotan & S. Herron	1–hole
J. Wilson & W. Murray bt. H. Johnston & J. Neville	4 & 3

SINGLES:

Wethered ½–with Ouimet	Halved
Tolley bt. Sweetser	4 & 3
Harris lost to Gardner	1–hole
Mackenzie lost to Rotan	5 & 4
Hope lost to Marston	6 & 5
Wilson bt. Herron	1–hole
Murray lost to Willing	2 & 1

RESULTS: USA, 6½. GB & IRE, 5½.

1924 GARDEN CITY, N.Y.

CAPTAINS: CYRIL TOLLEY AND ROBERT GARDINER

FOURSOMES:

E. Storey & W. Murray lost to M. Marston & R. Gardner	3 & 1
C. Tolley & C. Hezlet lost to J. Guilford & F. Quimet	2 & 1
Hon. M. Scott & R. Scott Jr. bt. R. Jones Jr. & W. Fownes Jr.	1–hole
T. Torrance & O. Bristowe lost to J. Sweetser & H. Johnston	4 & 3

SINGLES:

Tolley bt. Marston	1–hole
Hezlet lost to Jones Jr.	4 & 3
Murray lost to Evans Jr.	2 & 1
Storey lost to Ouimet	1–hole
Scott bt. Sweetser	7 & 6
Hope lost to Gardner	3 & 2
Torrance lost to Guilford	2 & 1
Kyle lost to Willing	3 & 2

RESULT: USA, 9. GB & IRE, 3.

1926 ST. ANDREWS

CAPTAINS: R. HARRIS AND ROBERT GARDINER

FOURSOMES:

R. Wethered & E. Holderness bt. F. Ouimet & J. Guilford	5 & 4
C. Folley & A. Jamieson Jr. lost to R. Jones Jr. & W. Gunn	4 & 3
R. Harris & Co. Hezlet lost to G. Von Elm & J. Sweetser	8 & 7
E. Storey & Hon. W. Brownlow lost to R. Gardner & R. MacKenzie	

SINGLES:

Tolley lost to Jones Jr.	12 & 11
Holderness lost to Sweetser	4 & 3
Wethered bt. Ouimet	5 & 4
Hezlet ½–with Von Elm	Halved
Harris bt. Guilford	2 & 1
Brownlow lost to Gunn	9 & 8
Storey bt. MacKenzie	2 & 1
Jamieson Jr. bt. Gardner	2 & 1

RESULT: USA, 6½. GB & IRE, 5½.

1928 CHICAGO GC, ILLINOIS

CAPTAINS: WILLIAM TWEDDELL AND BOBBY JONES

FOURSOMES:

T. Perkins & W. Tweddell lost to J. Sweetser & G. Von Elm	7 & 6
C. Hezlet & W. Hope lost to R. Jones Jr. & C. Evans Jr.	5 & 3
T. Torrance & E. Storey lost to F. Ouimet & H. Johnston	4 & 2
J. Beck & A. MacCullum lost to W. Gunn & R. MacKenzie	7 & 5

SINGLES:

Perkins lost to Jones Jr.	13 & 12
Tweddell lost to Von Elm	3 & 2
Hezlet lost to Ouimet	8 & 7
Hope lost to Sweetzer	5 & 4
Storey lost to Johnston	4 & 2
Torrance bt. Evans Jr.	1–hole
Hardman lost to Gunn	11 & 10
Martin lost to MacKenzie	2 & 1

RESULT: USA, 11. GB & IRE, 1.

1930 ROYAL ST. GEORGE'S, SANDWICH

CAPTAINS: ROGER WETHERED AND BOBBY JONES

FOURSOMES:

C. Tolley & R. Wethered bt. G. Von Elm & G. Voigt	2–holes
R. Hartley & T. Torrance lost to R. Jones Jr. & O. Willing	8 & 7
E. Holderness & J. Stout lost to R. MacKenzie & D. Moe	2 & 1
W. Campbell & J. Smith lost to H. Johnston & F. Ouimet	2 & 1

SINGLES:

Tolley lost to Johnston	5 & 4
Wethered lost to Jones Jr.	9 & 8
Hartley lost to Von Elm	3 & 2
Holderness lost to Voigt	10 & 8
Smith lost to Willing	2 & 1
Torrance bt. Ouimet	7 & 6
Stout lost to Moe	1–hole
Campbell lost to MacKenzie	6 & 5

RESULT: USA, 10. GB & IRE, 2.

1932 THE COUNTRY CLUB, BROOKLINE, MASS.

CAPTAINS: T. A. TORRANCE AND FRANCIS OUIMET

FOURSOMES:

R. Hartley & W. Harley lost to J. Sweetser & G. Voigt	7 & 6
T. Torrance & J. de Forest lost ot C. Seaver & G. Moreland	6 & 5
J. Stout & J. Burke lost to F. Ouimet & G. Dunlap Jr.	7 & 6
E. Fiddian & E. McRuvie lost to D. Moe & W. Howell	5 & 4

SINGLES:

Torrance ½–with Ouimet	Halved
Stout ½–with Sweetser	Halved
Hartley lost to Moreland	2 & 1
Burke ½–with Westland	Halved
Crawley bt. Voigt	1–hole
Hartley lost to McCarthy Jr.	3 & 2
Fiddian lost to Seaver	7 & 6
McRuvie lost to Dunlap Jr.	10 & 9

RESULT: USA, 9½. GB & IRE, 2½.

1934 ST. ANDREWS

CAPTAINS: HON. MICHAEL SCOTT AND FRANCIS OUIMET

FOURSOMES:

R. Wethered & C. Tolley lost to J. Goodman & L. Little Jr.	8 & 6
H. Bentley & E. Fiddian lost to G. Moreland & J. Westland	6 & 5
Hon. M. Scott & S. McKinlay lost to H. Egan & M. Marston	3 & 2
E. McRuvie & J. McLean bt. F. Ouimet & G. Dunlap Jr.	4 & 2

SINGLES:

Scott lost to Goodman	7 & 6
Tolley lost to Little Jr.	6 & 5
Crawley lost to Ouimet	5 & 4
McLean lost to Dunlap Jr.	4 & 3
Fiddian lost to Fischer	5 & 4
McKinlay lost to Moreland	3 & 1
McRuvie ½–with Westland	Halved
Torrance bt. Marston	4 & 3

RESULT: USA, 9½. GB & IRE, 2½.

1936 PINE VALLEY GC, N.J.

CAPTAINS: WILLIAM TWEDDELL AND FRANCIS OUIMET

FOURSOMES:

H. Thomson & H. Bentley lost to J. Goodman & A. Campbell	7 & 5
J. McLean & J. Langley lost to R. Smith & E. White	8 & 7
G. Peters & J. Dykes ½–with C. Yates & W. Emery	Halved
G. Hill & C. Ewing ½–with H. Givan & G. Voigt	Halved

SINGLES:

Thomson lost to Goodman	3 & 2
McLean lost to Campbell	5 & 4
Ewing lost to Fischer	8 & 7
Hill lost to Smith	11 & 9
Peters lost to Emery	1–hole
Dykes lost to Yates	8 & 7
Bentley ½–with Dunlap Jr.	Halved
Langley lost to White	6 & 5

RESULT: USA, 10½. GB & IRE, 1½.

1938 ST. ANDREWS

CAPTAINS: JOHN BECK AND FRANCIS OUIMET

FOURSOMES:

H. Bentley & J. Bruen ½–with J. Fisher & C. Kocsis	Halved
G. Peters & H. Thomson bt. J. Goodman & N. Ward	4 & 2
A. Kyle & C. Stowe lost to C. Yates & R. Billows	3 & 2
F. Pennick & L. Crawley bt. R. Smith & F. Haas Jr.	3 & 1

SINGLES:

Bruen lost to Yates	2 & 1
Thomson bt. Goodman	6 & 4
Crawley lost to Fischer	3 & 2
Stowe bt. Kocsis	2 & 1
Penninck lost to Ward	12 & 11
Ewing bt. Billows	1–hole
Peters bt. Smith	9 & 8
Kyle bt. Haas Jr.	5 & 4

RESULT: GB & IRE, 7½. USA, 4½.

1947 ST. ANDREWS

CAPTAINS: JOHN BECK AND FRANCIS OUIMET

FOURSOMES:

J. B. Carr & C. Ewing lost to S. Bishop & Skee Riegel	3 & 2
L. Crawley & P. Lucas bt. H. Ward & S. Quick	5 & 4
A. Kyle & J. Wilson lost to W. Turnesa & A. Kammer J.r	5 & 4
R. White & C. Stowe bt. F. Stranahan & R. Chapman	4 & 3

SINGLES:

Crawley lost to Ward	5 & 3
Carr bt. Bishop	5 & 3
Micklem lost to Riegel	6 & 5
Ewing lost to Turnesa	6 & 5
Stowe lost to Stranahan	2 & 1
White bt. Kammer Jr.	4 & 3
Wilson lost to Quick	8 & 6
Lucas lost to Chapman	4 & 3

RESULT: USA, 8. GB & IRE, 4.

1949 WINGED FOOT GC, N.Y.

CAPTAINS: LADDIE LUCAS AND FRANCIS OUIMET

FOURSOMES:

J. B. Carr & R. White bt. R. Billows & W. Turnesa	3 & 2
J. Bruen & S. McCready lost to C. Kocsis & F. Stranahan	2 & 1
C. Ewing & G. Micklem lost to S. Bishop & Skee Riegel	9 & 7
K. Thom & A. Perowne lost to J. Dawson & B. McCormick	8 & 7

SINGLES:

White bt. Turnesa	4 & 3
McCready lost to Stranahan	6 & 5
Bruen lost to Riegel	5 & 4
Carr lost to Dawson	5 & 3
Ewing lost to Coe	1–hole
Thom lost to Billows	2 & 1
Perowne lost to Kocsis	4 & 2
Micklem lost to McHale Jr	5 & 4

RESULT: USA, 10. GB & IRE, 2.

WALKER CUP RESULTS

1951 ROYAL BIRKDALE
CAPTAINS: RAYMOND OPPENHEIMER AND WILLIE TURNESA

FOURSOMES:

R. White & J. B. Carr ½—with F. Stranahan & W. Campbell	Halved
C. Ewing & J. Langley ½—with C. Coe & J. McHale Jr.	Halved
N. Kyle & I. Caldwell lost to R. Chapman & R. Knowles Jr.	1–hole
J. Bruen & J. Morgan lost to W. Turnesa & S. Urzetta	1–hole

SINGLES:

McCready lost to Urzetta	4 & 3
Carr bt. Stranahan	2 & 1
White bt. Coe	2 & 1
Langley lost to McHale Jr.	2–holes
Ewing lost to Campbell	5 & 4
Kyle bt. Turnesa	2–holes
Caldwell ½—with Paddock Jr.	Halved
Morgan lost to Chapman	7 & 6

RESULT: USA, 7½. GB & IRE, 4½.

1953 KITTANSETT GC, MASS
CAPTAINS: A. A. DUNCAN AND CHARLES YATES

FOURSOMES:

J. B. Carr & R. White lost to S. Urzetta & K. Venturi	6 & 4
J. Langley & A. Perowne lost to H. Ward Jr. & J. Westland	9 & 8
J. Wilson & R. MacGregor lost to J. Jackson & G. Littler	3 & 2
G. Micklem & J. Morgan bt. W. Campbell & C. Coe	4 & 3

SINGLES:

Carr lost to Ward Jr.	4 & 3
White bt. Chapman	1–hole
Micklem lost to Littler	5 & 3
MacGregor lost to Westland	7 & 5
Drew lost to Cherry	9 & 7
Wilson lost to Venturi	9 & 8
Morgan bt. Coe	3 & 2
Langley lost to Urzetta	3 & 2

RESULT: USA, 9. GB & IRE, 3.

1955 ST. ANDREWS
CAPTAINS: G. A. HILL AND BILL CAMPBELL

FOURSOMES:

J. B. Carr & R. White lost to H. Ward Jr. & D. Cherry	1–hole
G. Micklem & J. Morgan lost to W. Patton & R. Yost	2 & 1
I. Caldwell & B. Millward lost to J. Conrad & D. Morey	3 & 2
D. Blair & J. Cater lost to B. Cudd & J. Jackson	5 & 4

SINGLES:

White lost to Ward Jr.	6 & 5
Scrutton lost to Patton	2 & 1
Caldwell bt. Morey	1–hole
Carr lost to Cherry	5 & 4
Blair bt. Conrad	1–hole
Millward lost to Cudd	2–holes
Ewing lost to Jackson	6 & 4
Morgan lost to Yost	8 & 7

RESULT: USA, 10. GB & IRE, 2.

1957 MIMIKIHADA GC, MINNESOTA
CAPTAINS: GERALD MICKLEM AND CHARLES COE

FOURSOMES:

J. B. Carr & F. Deighton lost to R. Baxter Jr. & W. Patton	2 & 1
F. Bussell & P. Scrutton lost to W. Campbell & F. Taylor Jr.	4 & 3
R. Jack & D. Sewell lost to A. Blum & C. Kocsis	1·hole
A. Shepperson & G. Wolstenholme ½—with H. Robbins Jr. & M. Rudolph	Halved

SINGLES:

Jack lost to Patton	1–hole
Carr lost to Campbell	3 & 2
Thirlwell lost to Baxter Jr.	4 & 3
Deighton lost to Hyndman III	7 & 6
Bussell bt. Campbell	2 & 1
Sewell lost to Taylor Jr.	1–hole
Scrutton lost to Rudolph	3 & 2
Wolstenholme bt. Robbins Jr.	2 & 1

RESULT: USA, 8½. GB & IRE, 3½.

1959 MUIRFIELD GC, SCOTLAND
CAPTAINS: GERALD MICKLEM AND CHARLES COE

FOURSOMES:

R. Jack & D. Sewell lost to H. Ward Jr. & F. Taylor Jr.	1–hole
J. B. Carr & G. Wolstenholme lost to W. Hyndman III & T. Aaron	1–hole
M. Bonnallack & A. Perowne lost to W. Patton & C. Coe	9 & 8
M. Lunt & A. Shepperson lost to H. Wettlaufer & J. Nicklaus	2 & 1

SINGLES:

Carr bt Coe	2 & 1
Wolstenholme lost to Ward Jr	9 & 8
Jack bt Patton	5 & 3
Sewell lost to Hyndman III	4 & 3
Shepperson bt Aaron	2 & 1
Bonallack lost to Beman	2–holes
Lunt lost to Wettlaufer	6 & 5
Smith lost to Nicklaus	5 & 4

RESULT: USA, 9. GB & IRE, 3.

1961 SEATTLE GC, WASHINGTON
CAPTAINS: C. D. LAWRIE AND JACK WESTLAND

FOURSOMES:

J. Walker & G. Chapman lost to D. Beman & J. Nicklaus	6 & 5
D. Blair & M. Christmas lost to C. Coe & D. Cherry	1–hole
J. B. Carr & G. Huddy lost to W. Hyndman III & R. Gardner	4 & 3
M. Bonnallack & R. Shade lost to R. Cochran & E. Andrews	4 & 3

SINGLES:

Bonallack lost to Beman	3 & 2
Lunt lost to Coe	5 & 4
Walker lost to Taylor Jr.	3 & 2
Frame lost to Hyndman III	7 & 6
Carr lost to Nicklaus	6 & 4
Christmas bt. Smith	3 & 2
Shade lost to Gardner	1–hole
Blair lost to Cherry	5 & 4

RESULT: USA, 11. GB & IRE, 1.

1963 TURNBERRY
CAPTAINS: C. D. LAWRIE AND R. S. TUFTS

FOURSOMES (1):

M. Bonnallack & S. Murray bt. W. Patton & R. Sikes	4 & 3
J. B. Carr & G. Green lost to D. Gray & L. Harris	2–holes
M. Lunt & D. Sheahan lost to D. Beman & C. Coe	5 & 3
D. Madeley & R. Shade ½—with R. Gardner & E. Updegraff	Halved

SINGLES (1):

Murray bt. Beman	3 & 1
Christmas lost to Patton	3 & 2
Carr bt. Sikes	7 & 5
Sheahan bt. Harris	1–hole
Bonallack bt. Davies	1–hole
Saddler ½—with Coe	Halved
Shade bt. Gray	4 & 3
Lunt ½—with Smith	Halved

FOURSOMES (2):

M. Bonnallack & S. Murray lost to W. Patton & R. Sikes	1–hole
M. Lunt & D. Sheahan lost to D. Gray & L. Harris	3 & 2
C. Green & S. Saddler lost to R. Gardner & E. Updegraff	3 & 1
D. Madeley & R. Shade lost to D. Beman & C. Coe	3 & 2

SINGLES (2):

Murray lost to Patton	3 & 2
Sheahan bt. Davies	1–hole
Carr lost to Updegraff	4 & 3
Bonallack lost to Harris	3 & 2
Lunt lost to Gardner	3 & 2
Saddler ½—with Beman	Halved
Shade bt. Gray	2 & 1
Green lost to Coe	4 & 3

RESULT: USA, 14. GB & IRE, 10.

1965 BALTIMORE GC, MD.
CAPTAINS: JOE CARR AND JOHNNY FLETCHER

FOURSOMES (1):

M. Lunt & G. Cosh bt. W. Campbell & D. Gray	1–hole
M. Bonallack & C. Clark ½—with D. Beman & D. Allen	Halved
R. Foster & G. Clark lost to W. Patton & E. Tutwiler	5 & 4
P. Townsend & R. Shade bt. J. Hopkins & D. Eichelberger	2 & 1

SINGLES (1):

Bonallack lost to Campbell	6 & 5
Foster lost to Beman	2–holes
Shade bt. Gray	3 & 1
Clark bt. Hopkins	5 & 3
Townsend bt. Patton	3 & 2
Saddler bt. Morey	2 & 1
Lunt bt. Updegraff	2 & 1

FOURSOMES (2):

A. Saddler & R. Foster lost to W. Campbell & D. Gray	4 & 3
R. Shade & P. Townsend bt. D. Beman & D. Eichelberger	2 & 1
G. Cosh & M. Lunt lost to E. Tutwiler & W. Patton	2 & 1
C. Clark & M. Bonallack bt. D. Allen & D. Morey	2 & 1

SINGLES (2):

Foster lost to Campbell	3 & 2
Saddler lost to Beman	1–hole
Shade lost to Tutwiler	5 & 3
Cosh bt. Allen	4 & 3
Townsend lost to Gray	1–hole
Clark ½—with Hopkins	Halved
Bonallack lost to Eichelberger	5 & 3
Lunt lost to Patton	4 & 2

RESULT: GB & IRE, 13. USA, 12.

1967 ROYAL ST. GEORGE'S, SANDWICH
CAPTAINS: JOE CAR AND JESSE SWEETSER

FOURSOMES (1):

R. Shade & P. Oosterhuis ½—with R. Murphy Jr. & R. Cerrudo	Halved
R. Foster & A. Saddler lost to W. Campbell & W. Lewis	1–hole
M. Bonallack & M. Attenborough lost to D. Gray & E. Tutwiler	4 & 2
J. B. Carr & T. Craddock lost to R. Dickson & J. Grant	3 & 1

SINGLES (1):

Shade lost to Campbell	2 & 1
Foster lost to Murphy	2 & 1
Bonallack ½—with Gray	Halved
Attenborough lost to Cerrudo	4 & 3
Oosterhuis lost to Dickson	6 & 4
Craddock lost to Lewis	2 & 1
Pirie ½—with Allen	Halved
Saddler bt. Fleckman	3 & 2

FOURSOMES (2):

M. Bonallack & T. Craddock bt. R. Murphy & R. Cerrudo	2–holes
A. Saddler & A. Pirie lost to W. Campbell & W. Lewis	1–hole
R. Shade & P. Oosterhuis bt. D. Gray & E. Tutwiler	3 & 1
R. Foster & D. Millensted bt. D. Allen & M. Fleckman	2 & 1

SINGLES (2):

Shade lost to Campbell	3 & 2
Bonallack bt. Murphy	4 & 2
Saddler bt. Gray	3 & 2
Foster ½—with Cerrudo	Halved
Pirie lost to Grant	1–hole
Craddock bt. Lewis	5 & 4
Oosterhuis lost to Grant	1–hole
Millensted lost to Tutwiler	5 & 1

RESULT: USA, 15. GB & IRE, 9.

WALKER CUP RESULTS

1969 MILWAUKEE GC, WISCONSIN

CAPTAINS: MICHAEL BONALLACK AND BILLY JOE PATTON

FOURSOMES (1):

M. Bonallack & T. Craddock lost to M. Giles & S. Melynk	3 & 2
P. Benka & B. Critchley ½—with B. Fleisher & A. Miller	Halved
C. Green & A. Brooks bt. L. Wadkins & R. Siderowf	3 & 2
R. Foster & G. Marks lost to W. Hyndman & J. Inman	2 & 1

SINGLES (1):

Bonallack ½—with Fleisher	Halved
Green lost to Giles	1—hole
Critchley lost to Miller	1—hole
Tupling lost to Siderowf	6 & 5
Benka bt. McInyk	3 & 1
Marks bt. Wadkins	1—hole
M. King lost to J. Bohmann	2 & 1
Foster lost to E. Updegraff	6 & 5

FOURSOMES (2):

C. Green & A. Brooks ½—with M. Giles & S. McInyk	Halved
P. Benka & B. Critchley bt. B. Fleisher & A. Miller	2 & 1
R. Foster & M. King lost to R. Siderowf & L. Wadkins	6 & 5
M. Bonallack & P. Tupling bt. E. Updegraff & J. Bohmann	4 & 3

SINGLES (2):

Bonallack bt. Fleisher	5 & 4
Critchley ½—with Siderowf	Halved
King lost to Miller	1—hole
Craddock ½—with Giles	Halved
Benka lost to Inman	2 & 1
Brooks bt. Bohmann	4 & 3
Green ½—with Hyndman	Halved
Marks bt. Updegraff	3 & 2

RESULT: USA, 13. GB & IRE, 11.

1971 ST. ANDREWS

CAPTAINS: MICHAEL BONALLACK AND J. M. WINTERS

FOURSOMES (1):

M. Bonallack & W. Humphreys bt. L. Wadkins & J. Simons	1—hole
C. Green & R. Carr bt. S. McInyk & M. Giles	1—hole
D. Marsh & G. Macgregor bt. A. Miller & J. Farquhar	2 & 1
J. Macdonald & R. Foster bt. W. Campbell & T. Kite	2 & 1

SINGLES (1):

Green lost to Wadkins	1—hole
Bonallack lost to Giles	1—hole
Marks lost to Miller	1—hole
Macdonald lost to McInyk	3 & 2
Carr ½—with Hyndman	Halved
Humphreys lost to Gabrielsen	1—hole
Stuart bt. Farquhar	3 & 2
Foster lost to Kite	3 & 2

FOURSOMES (2):

G. Marks & C. Green lost to S. McInyk & M. Giles	1—hole
H. Stuart & R. Carr bt. W. Wadkins & J. Gabrielsen	1—hole
D. Marsh & M. Bonallack lost to A. Miller & J. Farquhar	5 & 4
J. Macdonald & R. Foster ½—with W. Campbell & T. Kite	Halved

SINGLES (2):

Bonallack lost to Wadkins	3 & 1
Stuart bt. Giles	2 & 1
Humphreys bt. McInyk	2 & 1
Green bt. Miller	1—hole
Carr bt. Simons	2—holes
Macgregor bt. Gabrielsen	1—hole
Marsh bt. Hyndman	1·hole
Marks lost to Kite	3 & 2

RESULT: GB & IRE, 13. USA, 11.

1973 THE COUNTRY CLUB, BROOKLINE, MASS.

CAPTAINS: DAVID MARSH AND JOHN SWEETSER

FOURSOMES (1):

M. King & P. Hedges ½—with M. Giles & G. Koch	Halved
H. Stuart & J. Davies lost to R. Siderowf & M. Pfeil	5 & 4
C. Green & W. Milne lost to D. Edwards & J. Ellis	2 & 1
R. Foster & T. Homer lost to M. West & D. Ballenger	2 & 1

SINGLES (1):

Stuart lost to Giles	5 & 4
Bonallack lost to Siderowf	4 & 2
Davies bt. Koch	1—hole
Clark bt West	2 & 1
Foster lost to Edwards	2—holes
King bt. Killian	1—hole
Green bt. Rodgers	1—hole
Milne bt. Pfeil	4 & 3

FOURSOMES (2):

T. Homer & R. Foster lost to M. Giles & G. Koch	7 & 5
H. Clark & J. Davies ½—with R. Siderowf & M. Pfeil	Halved
P. Hedges & M. King lost to D. Edwards & J. Ellis	2 & 1
H. Stuart & W. Milne lost to W. Rodgers & M. Killian	1—hole

SINGLES (2):

Stuart bt. Ellis	5 & 4
Davies bt. Siderowf	3 & 2
Homer lost to Edwards	2 & 1
Green ½—with Giles	Halved
King lost to West	1—hole
Milne bt. Killian	2 & 1
Hedges ½—with Koch	Halved
Clark lost to Pfeil	1—hole

RESULT: USA, 14. GB & IRE, 10.

1975 ST. ANDREWS

CAPTAINS: DAVID MARSH AND ED UPDEGRAFF

FOURSOMES (1):

M. James and G. Eyles bt. J. Pate and R. Siderowf	1—hole
J. Davies and M. Poxon lost to G. Burns & C. Stadler	5 & 4
C. Green and H. Stuart lost to J. Haas & C. Strange	2 & 1
C. Macgregor and I. Hutcheon lost to M. Giles and G. Koch	5 & 4

SINGLES (1):

James bt. Pate	2 & 1
Davies ½—with Strange	Halved
P. Mulcare bt. Siderowf	3 & 2
Stuart lost to Koch	3 & 2
Poxon lost to J. Grace	3 & 1
Hutcheon ½—with W. Campbell	Halved
Eyles lost to Haas	2 & 1
Macgregor lost to Giles	3 & 2

FOURSOMES (2):

Mulcare & Hutcheon bt. Pate & Siderowf	1—hole
Green & Stuart lost to Burns & Stadler	1—hole
James & Eyles bt. Campbell & Grace	5 & 3
Hedges & Davies lost to Haas & Strange	3 & 2

SINGLES (2):

Hutcheon bt. Pate	3 & 2
Mulcare lost to Strange	4 & 3
James lost to Koch	5 & 4
Davies bt. Burns	2 & 1
Green lost to Grace	2 & 1
Macgregor lost to Stadler	3 & 2
Eyles lost to Campbell	2 & 1
Hedges ½—with Giles	Halved

RESULT: USA, 15. GB & IRE, 8½.

1977 SHINNECOCK HILLS, N.Y.

CAPTAINS: SANDY SADDLER AND R. W. OEHMIT

FOURSOMES (1):

J. Fought & V. Heafner bt. P. McEvoy & A. Lyle	4 & 3
S. Simpson & L. Miller bt. J. Davies & M. Kelley	5 & 4
R. Siderowf & G. Hallberg lost to I. Hutcheon & P. Deeble	1—hole
J. Sigel & M. Brannan bt. A. Brodie & S. Martin	1—hole

SINGLES (1):

Miller bt. McEvoy	2—holes
Fought bt. Hutcheon	4 & 3
Simpson bt. G. Murray	7 & 6
Heafner bt. Davies	4 & 3
B. Sander lost to Brodie	4 & 3
Hallberg lost to Martin	3 & 2
F. Ridley bt. Lyle	2—holes
Sigel bt. P. McKellar	5 & 3

FOURSOMES (2):

Fought & Heafner bt. Hutcheon & Deeble	4 & 3
Miller & Simpson bt. McEvoy & Davies	2—holes
Siderowf & Sander lost to Brodie & Martin	6 & 4
Ridley & Brannan lost to Murray & Kelley	4 & 3

SINGLES (2):

Miller bt. Martin	1—hole
Fought bt. Davies	2 & 1
Sander lost to Brodie	2 & 1
Hallberg bt. McEvoy	4 & 3
Siderowf lost to Kelley	2 & 1
Brannan lost to Hutcheon	2—holes
Ridley bt. Lyle	5 & 3
Sigel bt. Deeble	1—hole

RESULT: USA, 16. GB & IRE, 8.

1979 MUIRFIELD, SCOTLAND

CAPTAINS: RODNEY FOSTER AND R. L. SIDEROWF

FOURSOMES (1):

P. McEvoy & B. Marchbank lost to S. Hock and J. Sigel	1—hole
G. Goodwin & I. Hutcheon bt. M. West & H. Sutton	2—holes
G. Brand & M. Kelley lost to D. Fischesser & J. Holtgrieve	1—hole
A. Brodie & I. Carslaw bt. G. Moody & M. Gove	2 & 1

SINGLES (1):

McEvoy ½—with Sigel	Halved
Davies lost to Clark	8 & 7
Hutcheon lost to Holtgrieve	6 & 4
Buckley lost to Hoch	9 & 7
Marchbank bt. Peck	1—hole
Godwin bt. Moody	3 & 2
Kelley bt. Fischesser	3 & 2
Brodie lost to Gove	3 & 2

FOURSOMES (2):

Goodwin & Brand lost to Hock and Sigel	4 & 3
McEvoy & Marchbank bt. Fischesser and Holtgrieve	2 & 1
Kelley & Hutcheon ½—with West & Sutton	Halved
Carslaw & Brodie ½—with D. Clarke and Peck	Halved

SINGLES (2):

McEvoy lost to Hoch	3 & 1
Brand lost to Clarke	2 & 1
Godwin lost to Gove	3 & 2
Hutcheon lost to Peck	2 & 1
Brodie bt. West	3 & 2
Kelley lost to Moody	3 & 2
Marchbank lost to Sutton	3 & 1
Carslaw lost to Sigel	2 & 1

RESULT: USA, 15½. GB & IRE, 8½.

WALKER CUP RESULTS

1981 CYPRESS POINT, CALIFORNIA
CAPTAINS: RODNEY FOSTER AND J. GABRIELSON

FOURSOMES (1):

H. Sutton & J. Sigel lost to P. Walton & R. Rafferty	4 & 2
J. Holtgrieve & F. Fuhrer bt. R. Chapman & P. McEvoy	1–hole
B. Lewis & D. von Tacky bt. P. Deeble & I. Hutcheon	2 & 1
R. Commans & C. Pavin bt. D. Evans & P. Way	5 & 4

SINGLES (1):

Sutton bt. Rafferty	
J. Rassett bt. C. Dalgleish	1–hole
Commans lost to Walton	1–hole
Lewis lost to Chapman	2 & 1
Pavin bt. Hutcheon	3 & 4
J. Mudd bt. J. Godwin	1–hole
von Tacky lost to Way	3 & 1
Sigel bt. McEvoy	4 & 2

FOURSOMES (2):

Sutton & Sigel lost to Chapman & Way	1–hole
Holtgrieve & Fuhrer lost to Walton & Rafferty	6 & 4
Lewis & von Tacky lost to D. Evans & Dalgleish	3 & 2
Rassett & Mudd bt. Hutcheon & Godwin	5 & 4

SINGLES (2):

Sutton lost to Chapman	1–hole
Holtgrieve bt. Rafferty	2 & 1
Fuhrer bt. Walton	4 & 2
Sigel bt. Way	6 & 5
Mudd bt. Dalgleish	7 & 5
Commans ½–with Godwin	Halved
Rassett bt. Deeble	4 & 3
Pavin ½–with Evans	Halved

RESULT: USA, 15. GB & IRE, 9.

1983 HOYLAKE
CAPTAINS: CHARLES GREEN AND JAY SIGEL

FOURSOMES (1):

M. Lewis & M. Thompson lost to B. Lewis & J. Holtgrieve	7 & 6
G. MacGregor & P. Walton bt. J. Sigel & R. Fehr	3 & 1
L. Mann & A. Oldcorn bt. W. Hoffer & D. Tentis	5 & 4
S. Keppler & A. Pierse lost to W. Wood & B. Faxon	3 & 1

SINGLES (1):

P. Parkin bt. N. Crosby	6 & 4
Mann lost to Holtgrieve	6 & 5
Oldcorn bt. B. Tuten	4 & 3
Walton bt. Sigel	1–hole
Keppler lost to Fehr	1–hole
D. Carrick lost to Faxon	3 & 1
Macgregor ½–with Wood	Halved
Pierse lost to Lewis	3 & 1

FOURSOMES (2):

Macgregor & Walton lost to Crosby & Hoffer	2–holes
Parkin & M. Thompson bt. Faxon & Wood	1–hole
Mann & Oldcorn lost to Lewis & Holtgrieve	1–hole
Keppler & Pierse ½–with Sigel & Fehr	Halved

SINGLES (2):

Walton bt. Wood	2 & 1
Parkin lost to Faxon	3 & 2
Macgregor lost to Fehr	2 & 1
Thompson lost to Tuten	3 & 2
Mann ½–with Tentis	Halved
Keppler lost to Lewis	6 & 5
Oldcorn bt. Holtgrieve	3 & 2
Carrick lost to Sigel	3 & 1

RESULT: USA, 13½. GB & IRE, 10½.

1985 PINE VALLEY GC, N.J.
CAPTAINS: CHARLES GREEN AND JAY SIGEL

FOURSOMES (1):

C. Montgomerie & G. Macgregor lost to S. Verplank & J. Sigel	1–hole
J. Hawksworth & G. McGimpsey bt. D. Waldorf & S. Randolph	4 & 3
P. Baker & P. McEvoy bt. R. Sonnier & J. Haas	6 & 5
C. Bloice & S. Stephen ½–with M. Podolak & D. Love	Halved

SINGLES (1):

McGimpsey lost to Verplank	2 & 1
P. Mayo lost to Randolph	5 & 4
Hawksworth ½–with Sonnier	Halved
Montgomerie lost to Sigel	5 & 4
McEvoy bt. Lewis	2 & 1
Macgregor bt. C. Burroughs	2–holes
D. Gilford lost to Waldorf	4 & 2
Stephen bt. Haas	2 & 1

FOURSOMES (2):

Mayo & Montgomerie ½–with Verplank & Sigel	Halved
Hawksworth & McGimpsey lost to Randolph & Haas	3 & 2
Baker & McEvoy lost to Lewis & Burroughs	2 & 1
Bloice & Stephen lost to Podolak & Love	3 & 2

SINGLES (2):

McGimpsey ½–with Randolph	Halved
Montgomerie lost to Verplank	1–hole
Hawksworth bt. Sigel	4 & 3
McEvoy lost to Love	5 & 3
Baker bt. Sonnier	5 & 4
Macgregor bt. Burroughs	3 & 2
Bloice lost to Lewis	4 & 3
Stephen bt. Waldorf	2 & 1

RESULT: USA, 13. GB & IRE, 11.

1987 SUNNINGDALE
CAPTAINS: S. RIDLEY AND GEOFFREY MARKS

FOURSOMES (1):

Alexander & Mayfair bt. Montgomerie & Shaw	5 & 4
Kite & Mattiace bt. Curry & Mayo	2 & 1
Lewis & Loeffler bt. Macgregor & Robinson	2 & 1
Sigel & Andrade bt. McHenry & Girvan	3 & 2

SINGLES (1):

B. Alexander lost to D. Curry	2–holes
Sorenson lost to C. Montgomerie	3 & 2
J. Sigel bt. Eggo	3 & 2
B. Andrade bt. J. Robinson	7 & 5
Montgomery bt. J. McHenry	1–hole
B. Lewis bt. P. Girvan	3 & 2
B. Mayfair bt. D. Carrick	2–holes
C. Kite lost to G. Shaw	1–hole

FOURSOMES (2):

Lewis & Loeffler bt. Curry & Carrick	4 & 3
Kite & Mattiace bt. Montgomerie & Shaw	1–hole
Sorenson & Montgomery bt. Mayo & Macgregor	4 & 3
Siegel & Andrade lost to McHenry & Robinson	4 & 2

SINGLES (2):

B. Alexander bt. D. Curry	5 & 4
B. Andrade lost to C. Montgomerie	4 & 2
B. Loeffler lost to J. McHenry	3 & 2
Sorenson ½–with G. Shaw	Halved
L. Mattiace lost to J. Robinson	1–hole
B. Lewis bt. D. Carrick	3 & 2
J. Sigel bt. P. Girvan	6 & 5
B. Mayfair lost to Eggo	1–hole

RESULT: USA, 16½. GB & IRE, 7½.

CURTIS CUP

1932 WENTWORTH
CAPTAINS: JOYCE WETHERED AND MARION HOLLINS

FOURSOMES:

J. Wethered & W. Morgan lost to G. Collett Vare & Mrs. O. S. Hill	1–hole
E. Wilson & J. B. Watson lost to V. Van Wic & H. Hicks	2 & 1
M. Gourlay & D. Park lost to M. Orcutt & Mrs. L. D. Cheney	1–hole

SINGLES:

J. Wethered bt. G. Collett Vare	6 & 4
E. Wilson bt. H. Hicks	2 & 1
W. Morgan lost to V. Van Wic	2 & 1
D. Fishwick bt. M. Orcutt	4 & 3
M. Gourlay ½–with Mrs. O. S. Hill	Halved
E. Corlett lost to Mrs. L. D. Cheney	4 & 3

RESULT: USA, 5½. GB & IRE, 3½.

1934 CHEVY CHASE, MD.
CAPTAINS: DORIS CHAMBERS AND GLENNA COLLETT VARE

FOURSOMES:

M. Gourlay & P. Barton ½–with V. Van Wic & C. Glutting	Halved
D. Fishwick & W. Morgan lost to M. Orcutt & Mrs. L. D. Cheney	2–holes
D. Plumpton & Mrs. J. B. Walker bt. Mrs. O. S. Hill & L. Robinson	2 & 1

SINGLES:

D. Fishwick lost to V. Van Wic	2 & 1
M. Gourlay lost to M. Orcutt	4 & 2
P. Barton lost to Mrs. L. D. Cheney	7 & 5
W. Morgan lost to C. Glutting	3 & 2
D. Plumpton lost to Mrs. O. S. Hill	3 & 2
Mrs. J. Walker bt. Mrs. Goldthwaite	3 & 2

RESULT: USA, 6½. GB & IRE, 2½.

1936 GLENEAGLES
CAPTAINS: DORIS CHAMBERS AND GLENNA COLLETT VARE

FOURSOMES:

W. Morgan & M. Ross Garon ½–with G. Collett Vare & P. Berg	Halved
P. Barton & Mrs. J. B. Walker lost to M. Orcutt & Mrs. L. D. Cheney	2 & 1
J. Anderson & Mrs. A. M. Holm bt. Mrs. O. S. Hill & C. Glutting	3 & 2

SINGLES:

Morgan lost to Collett Vare	3 & 2
Holm bt. Berg	4 & 3
Barton lost to Glutting	1–hole
Walker bt. Orcutt	1–hole
Anderson bt. Cheney	1–hole
Ross Garon bt. Hill	7 & 5

RESULT: GB & IRE, 4½. USA, 4½.

1938 ESSEX COUNTRY CLUB, MASS.
CAPTAINS: MRS. WALLACE–WILLIAMS AND FRANCES E. STREBBINS

FOURSOMES:

Mrs. M. Holm & C. Tiernan bt. Mrs. A. Page Jr. & M. Orcutt	2–holes
J. Anderson & E. Corlett bt. G. Collett Vare & P. Berg	1–hole
Mrs. J. B. Walker & P. Wade ½–with M. Miley & K. Hemphill	Halved

SINGLES:

Holm lost to Page Jr.	6 & 5
Anderson lost to Berg	1–hole
Corlett lost to Miley	2 & 1
Walker lost to Collett Vare	2 & 1
Tiernan beat Orcutt	2 & 1
Baird lost to Glutting	1–hole

RESULT: USA, 5½. GB & IRE, 3½.

1948 ROYAL BIRKDALE
CAPTAINS: DORIS E. CHAMBERS AND GLENNA COLLETT VARE

FOURSOMES:

J. Gordon & J. Donald bt. L. Suggs & G. Lenczyk	
P. Garvey & Z. Bolton lost to G. Collett Vare & D. Kirby	4 & 3
M. Ruttle & Mrs. V. Reddan lost to D. Kielty & Mrs. J. A. Page Jr.	5 & 4

SINGLES:

Garvey ½–with Suggs	Halved
Donald bt. Kirby	2–holes
J. Gordon lost to Lenczyk	5 & 3
Holm lost to Page Jr.	3 & 2
Ruttle lost to Riley	3 & 2
Bolton lost to Kielty	2 & 1

RESULT: USA, 6½. GB & IRE, 2½.

CURTIS CUP

1950 COUNTRY CLUB OF BUFFALO, N.Y.
CAPTAINS: MRS. A. C. CRITCHLEY AND
GLENNA COLLETT VARE

FOURSOMES:

J. Donald & Mrs. G. Valentine lost to D. Porter & B. Hanson	3 & 2
F. Stephens & E. Price bt. Sigel & P. Kirk	1–hole
P. Garvey & J. Bisgood lost to D. Kielty & D. Kirby	6 & 5

SINGLES:

Stephens ½–with Porter	Halved
Valentine lost to Riley	7 & 6
Donald lost to Hanson	6 & 5
Garvey lost to Kielty	3 & 1
Bisgood lost to Kirk	1–hole
Price lost to Lenczyk	5 & 4

RESULT: USA, 7½. GB & IRE, 1½.

1952 MUIRFIELD
CAPTAINS: LADY KATHERINE CAIRNS AND
MRS. FRANK GOLDTHWAITE

FOURSOMES:

J. Donald & E. Price bt. D. Kirby & G. DeMoss	
F. Stephens & Mrs. G. Valentine lost to C. Doran & M. Lindsay	6 & 4
M. Paterson & P. Garvey bt. P. Riley & P. O'Sullivan	2 & 1

SINGLES:

Donald lost to Kirby	1–hole
Stephens bt. Lindsay	2 & 1
Paterson lost to Riley	6 & 4
Bisgood bt. Murray	6 & 5
Garvey lost to Doran	3 & 2
Price bt. DeMoss	3 & 2

RESULT: GB & IRE, 5. USA, 4.

1954 MERION GC. PA.
CAPTAINS: MRS. JOHN BECK AND
MRS. HARRISON FLIPPIN

FOURSOMES:

F. Stephens & E. Price lost to M. L. Faulk & P. Riley	6 & 4
Mrs. G. Valentine & P. Garvey lost to C. Doran & P. Lesser	6 & 5
Mrs. R. T. Peel & J. Robertson lost to D. Kirby & B. Romack	6 & 5

SINGLES:

Stephens bt. Faulk	1–hole
Bisgood lost to Doran	4 & 3
Price lost to Riley	9 & 8
Garvey bt. Kirby	3 & 1
Valentine lost to De Moss Smith	4 & 3
Robertson bt. Ziske	3 & 1

RESULT: USA, 6. GB & IRE, 3.

1956 PRINCE'S GC. SANDWICH
CAPTAINS: MRS. SLOAN BOLTON AND
MRS. H. FLIPPIN

FOURSOMES:

Mrs. G. Valentine & P. Garvey lost to P. Lesser & M. Smith	2 & 1
Mrs. P. Smith & E. Price beat Riley & B. Romack	5 & 3
J. Robertson & V. Anstey lost to M. A. Downey & P. J. Cudone	6 & 4

SINGLES:

Valentine bt. Lesser	6 & 4
Garvey lost to Smith	9 & 8
Smith bt. Riley	1–hole
Robertson lost to Romack	6 & 4
Ward bt. Downey	4 & 3
Price bt. Nelson	7 & 6

RESULT: GB & IRE, 5. USA, 4.

1958 BRAE BURN GC. MASS.
CAPTAINS: DAISY FERGUSON AND
MRS. CHARLES DENNEHY

FOURSOMES:

Mrs. A. Bonallack & E. Price bt. B. Romack & P. Riley	2 & 1
J. Robertson & F. Smith bt. J. A. Gunderson & A. Quast	3 & 2
B. Jackson & Mrs. G. Valentine lost to B. McIntire & A. Johnstone	6 & 5

SINGLES:

Valentine lost to Gunderson	2–holes
Bonallack ½–with McIntire	Halved
Price lost to Quast	4 & 2
Robertson bt. Johnstone	3 & 2
Jackson lost to Romack	4 & 2
Smith bt. Riley	2–holes

RESULT: GB & IRE, 4½. USA, 4½.

1960 LINDRICK
CAPTAINS: MAUREEN GARRETT AND
MRS. HENRI PRUNARET

FOURSOMES:

A. Bonallack & E. Price bt. J. A. Gunderson & B. McIntire	1–hole
B. McCorkindale & J. Robertson lost to J. Eller & A. Quast	4 & 2
R. Porter & F. Smith lost to J. Goodwin & A. C. Johnstone	3 & 2

SINGLES:

Price ½–with McIntire	Halved
Bonallack lost to Gunderson	2 & 1
Robertson lost to Quast	2–holes
Garvey lost to Eller	4 & 3
McCorkindale lost to Bell	8 & 7
Porter bt. Goodwin	1–hole

RESULT: USA, 6½. GB & IRE. 2½.

1962 BROADMOOR. COLORADO
CAPTAINS: FRANCIS SMITH AND POLLY RILEY

FOURSOMES:

A. Bonallack & Mrs. M. Spearman lost to A. Decker & B. McIntire	7 & 5
A. Irvin & S. Vaughan lost to C. A. Creed & J. A. Gunderson	4 & 3
Mrs. A. Frearson & R. Porter beat J. Ashley & A. Johnstone	8 & 7

SINGLES:

Spearman lost to Decker	5 & 4
Bonallack lost to Gunderson	2 & 1
Frearson bt. Bell	8 & 7
Roberts lost to Preuss	1–hole
Bonallack lost to Creed	6 & 5
Vaughan lost to McIntire	5 & 4

RESULT: USA, 8. GB & IRE, 1.

1964 ROYAL PORTCAWL
CAPTAINS: ELSIE CORLETT AND
MRS. T. W. HAWES

FOURSOMES (1):

Mrs. M. Spearman & A. Bonallack bt. B. McIntire & P. Preuss	2 & 1
B. Jackson & S. Armitage lost to C. Sorenson & B. White	8 & 6
S. Vaughan & R. Porter bt. J. A. Gunderson & N. Roth	3 & 2

SINGLES (1):

Spearman ½–with McIntire	Halved
Bonallack lost to Gunderson	6 & 5
Lawrence lost to Conley	1–hole
Greenhalgh lost to White	3 & 2
Jackson bt. Sorenson	4 & 2
Porter bt. Roth	1–hole

FOURSOMES (2):

Mrs. M. Spearman & A. Bonallack bt. B. McIntire & P. Preuss	6 & 5
S. Armitage & B. Jackson lost to J. A. Gunderson & N. Roth	2–holes
R. Porter & S. Vaughan ½–with C. Sorenson & B. F. White	Halved

SINGLES (2):

Spearman ½–with Gunderson	Halved
Lawrence lost to McIntire	4 & 2
Greenhalgh bt. Preuss	5 & 2
Jackson lost to Conley	1–hole
Bonallack lost to White	3 & 2
Porter lost to Sorenson	3 9 2

RESULT: USA, 10½. GB & IRE, 7½.

1966 CASCADES GC. HOT SPRINGS. VA.
CAPTAINS: MRS. S. M. BOLTON AND
DOROTHY G. PORTER

FOURSOMES (1):

A. Bonallack & S. Armitage lost to J. Ashley & P. Preuss	1–hole
Mrs. I. C. Robertson & J. Hastings ½–with A. Q. Welts & B. McIntire	Halved
E. Chadwick & P. Tredinnick lost to B. Boddie & C. Sorenson Flenniken	1–hole

SINGLES (1):

Robertson lost to Ashley	1–hole
Armitage ½–with Welts	Halved
Bonallack lost to Boddie	3 & 2
Chadwick lost to Roth Syms	2–holes
Burke bt. Sigel Wilson	3 & 1
Fowler lost to Sorenson Flenniken	3 & 2

FOURSOMES (2):

A. Bonallack & S. Armitage lost to J. Ashley & P. Preuss	3 & 1
E. Chadwick & L. Burke bt. A. Q. Welts & B. McIntire	1–hole
Mrs. I. C. Robertson & J. Hastings lost to B. Boddie & C. Sorenson Flenniken	2 & 1

SINGLES (2):

Bonallack bt. Ashley	2 & 1
Robertson ½–with Welts	Halved
Armitage lost to Boddie	3 & 2
Tredinnick ½–with Roth Syms	Halved
Chadwick lost to Preuss	3 & 2
Burke lost to Sorenson Flenniken	2 & 1

RESULT: USA, 13. GB & IRE, 5.

1966 ROYAL CO. DOWN GC. IRELAND
CAPTAINS: MRS. S. M. BOLTON AND
MRS. ROBERT MONSTED

FOURSOMES (1):

Mrs. I. C. Robertson & A. Irvin bt. S. Hamlin & A. Q. Welts	6 & 5
M. Pickard & V. Saunders bt. M. L. Dill & P. Conley	3 & 2
A. Howard & P. Tredinnick lost to P. Preuss & J. Ashley	1–hole

SINGLES (1):

Irvin bt. Welts	3 & 2
Saunders lost to Hamlin	1–hole
Robertson lost to Albers	1–hole
Jackson ½–with Conley	Halved
Oxley ½–with Preuss	Halved
Pickard bt. Ashley	2–holes

FOURSOMES (2):

Mrs. I. C. Roberts & A. Irvin ½–with M. L. Dill & P. Conley	
M. Pickard & V. Saunders lost to S. Hamlin & A. Q. Welts	2 & 1
D. Oxley & P. Tredinnick lost to P. Preuss & J. Ashley	5 & 4

SINGLES (2):

Irvin bt. Hamlin	3 & 2
Robertson ½–with Welts	Halved
Saunders ½–with Albers	Halved
Pickard lost to Conley	1–hole
Howard lost to Dill	4 & 2
Jackson lost to Preuss	2 & 1

RESULT: USA, 10½. GB & IRE, 7½.

CURTIS CUP

1970 BRAE BURN GC, MASS.
CAPTAINS: JEANNE BISGOOD AND
MRS. PHILIP CUDONE

FOURSOMES (1):

D. Oxley & M. McKenna bt. S. Hamlin & J. Bastanchury	4 & 3
Mrs. I. C. Robertson & A. Irvin lost to P. Preuss & M. Wilkinson	4 & 3
M. Everard & J. Greenhalgh bt. C. Hill & J. Fassinger	5 & 3

SINGLES (1):

Oxley lost to Bastanchury	5 & 3
Irvin lost to Wilkinson	1–hole
Robertson ½–with Hamlin	Halved
McKenna bt. Preuss	4 & 2
Pickard lost to Hager	5 & 4
Greenhalgh lost to Dye Jr.	1–hole

FOURSOMES (2):

D. Oxley & M. McKenna lost to P. Preuss & M. Wilkinson	6 & 4
Mrs. I. C. Robertson & A. Irvin lost to S. Hamlin & J. Bastanchury	1–hole
M. Everard & J. Greenhalgh ½–with C. Hill & Mrs. P. Dye Jr.	Halved

SINGLES (2):

Oxley ½–with Hamlin	Halved
Irvin lost to Bastanchury	4 & 3
Robertson lost to Preuss	1–hole
Greenhalgh bt. Wilkinson	6 & 4
Everard bt. Hager	4 & 3
McKenna lost to Hill	2 & 1

RESULT: USA, 11½. GB & IRE, 6½.

1972 WESTERN GAILES
CAPTAINS: MRS. F. SMITH & MRS. J. CRAWFORD

FOURSOMES (1):

M. Everard & B. Huke lost to L. Baugh & Mrs. M. Kirouac	2 & 1
Mrs. I. C. Robertson & Mrs. D. Frearson lost to J. Booth & B. McIntire	2 & 1
M. Walker & M. McKenna bt. B. Barry & H. Stacy	1–hole

SINGLES (1):

Walker ½–with Baugh	Halved
Robertson lost to Booth	3 & 1
Everard lost to Kirouac	4 & 3
Oxley lost to McIntire	4 & 3
Phillips bt. Smith	2–holes
McKenna lost to Barry	2 & 1

FOURSOMES (2):

M. Walker & M. McKenna bt. L. Baugh & Mrs. M. Kirouac	3 & 2
M. Everard & B. Huke lost to J. Booth & B. McIntire	5 & 4
Mrs. I. C. Robertson & Mrs. D. Frearson ½–with B. Barry & H. Stacey	Halved

SINGLES (2):

Robertson lost to Baugh	6 & 5
Everard bt. McIntire	6 & 5
Walker bt. Booth	1–hole
McKenna bt. Kirouac	3 & 1
Frearson lost to Smith	3 & 1
Phillips lost to Barry	3 & 1

RESULT: USA, 10. GB & IRE, 8.

1974 SAN FRANCISCO GC, CALIFORNIA
CAPTAINS: MRS. BELLE ROBERTSON AND
MRS. ALLISON CHOATE

FOURSOMES (1):

M. McKenna & J. Greenhalgh ½–with C. Semple & C. Hill	Halved
J. Lee-Smith & C. Le Feuvre lost to A. Sander & J. Booth	6 & 5
M. Walker & M. Everard bt. Budke & Lauer	5 & 4

SINGLES (1):

Walker bt. Semple	2 & 1
McKenna lost to Booth	5 & 3
Everard lost to Massey	1–hole
Lee–Smith lost to Lauer	6 & 4
Greenhalgh lost to Barry	1–hole
Perkins ½–with Hill	Halved

FOURSOMES (2):

M. McKenna & M. Walker lost to A. Sander & J. Booth	5 & 4
M. Everard & C. Le Feuvre lost to M. Budke & B. Lauer	5 & 3
J. Greenhalgh & T. Perkins bt. C. Semple & C. Hill	3 & 2

SINGLES (2):

Everard lost to Sander	4 & 3
Greenhalgh lost to Booth	7 & 5
Le Feuvre lost to Massey	6 & 5
Walker lost to Semple	2 & 1
Perkins lost to Budke	5 & 4
McKenna bt. Lauer	2 & 1

RESULT: USA, 13. GB & IRE, 5.

1976 ROYAL LYTHAM & ST. ANNE'S
CAPTAINS: BELLE ROBERTSON AND
BARBARA McINTIRE

FOURSOMES (1):

M. McKenna and J. Greenhalgh lost to B. Daniel and C. Hill	3 & 2
Mrs. D. Henson and S. Cadden lost to D. Massey and D. Horton	6 & 5
A. Irvin and T. Perkins lost to Mrs. N. Syms and C. Semple	3 & 2

SINGLES (1):

Irvin lost to Daniel	4 & 3
Henson bt. Hill	1–hole
Cadden lost to Lopez	3 & 1
McKenna lost to Syms	1–hole
Perkins lost to Massey	1–hole
Greenhalgh ½–with Barrow	Halved

FOURSOMES (2):

A. Irvin and S. Cadden lost to B. Daniel and C. Hill	4 & 3
Mrs. D. Henson and T. Perkins bt. C. Semple and Mrs. N. Syms	2 & 1
M. McKenna and Mrs. A. Stant lost to N. Lopez and B. Barrow	4 & 2

SINGLES (2):

Henson lost to Daniel	3 & 2
Greenhalgh bt. Syms	2 & 1
Cadden lost to Horton	6 & 5
Lee-Smith lost to Massey	3 & 2
Perkins bt. Hill	1–hole
McKenna bt. Semple	1–hole

RESULT: USA, 11½. GB & IRE, 6½.

1978 APAWAMIS GC, N.Y.
CAPTAINS: CAROL COMBOY AND
HELEN SIGEL WILSON

FOURSOMES (1):

J. Greenhalgh and V. Marvin bt. B. Daniel and B. Goldsmith	3 & 2
M. Everard and M. Thompson bt. C. Hill and L. Smith	2 & 1
T. Perkins & M. McKenna ½–with P. Cornett & Carolyn Hill	Halved

SINGLES (1):

Marvin lost to Daniel	5 & 4
Everard bt. Uihlein	7 & 6
Uzielli lost to Smith	4 & 3
Greenhalgh lost to Hill	2 & 1
Caldwell ½–with Carolyn Hill	Halved
Perkins lost to Oliver	2 & 1

FOURSOMES (2):

M. Everard and M. Thomson lost to Cynthia Hill and L. Smith	1–hole
T. Perkins and M. McKenna lost to B. Goldsmith and B. Daniel	1–hole
J. Greenhalgh & V. Marvin lost to Mrs. N. Uihlein & Mrs. J. Oliver	4 & 3

SINGLES (2):

McKenna lost to Daniel	2 & 1
Caldwell lost to Cornett	3 & 2
Thomson bt. Cynthia Hill	2 & 1
Perkins lost to Smith	2–holes
Greenhalgh ½–with Oliver	Halved
Everard ½–with Uihlein	Halved

RESULT: USA, 12. GB & IRE, 6.

1980 ST. PIERRE GC, CHEPSTOW
CAPTAINS: CAROL COMBOY AND
NANCY ROTH SYMS

FOURSOMES (1):

M. McKenna & C. Nesbitt ½–with L. Smith & T. Moody	Halved
Mrs. T. Thomas & G. Steward lost to P. Sheehan & L. Castillo	5 & 3
M. Madill & Mrs. C. Caldwell ½–with Mrs. J. Oliver & C. Semple	Halved

SINGLES (1):

McKenna lost to Sheehan	3 & 2
Nesbitt ½–with Smith	Halved
Connachan lost to Goldsmith	2–holes
Madill lost to Semple	4 & 3
Moore ½–with Hafeman	Halved
Caldwell lost to Oliver	1–hole

FOURSOMES (2):

Mrs. C. Caldwell & M. Madill lost to P. Sheehan & L. Castillo	3 & 2
C. Nesbitt & M. McKenna lost to L. Smith & T. Moody	6 & 5
Mrs. T. Thomas & L. Moore lost to Mrs. J. Oliver & C. Semple	1–hole

SINGLES (2):

Madill lost to Sheehan	5 & 4
McKenna bt. Castillo	5 & 4
Connachan lost to Hafeman	6 & 5
Stewart bt. Smith	5 & 4
Moore bt. Goldsmith	1–hole
Thomas lost to Semple	4 & 3

RESULT: USA, 13. GB & IRE, 5.

1982 DENVER, COLORADO
CAPTAINS: MAIRE O'DONNELL AND
BETTY PROBASCO

FOURSOMES (1):

Mrs. Robertson & M. McKenna lost to J. Inkster & C. Semple	5 & 4
K. Douglas & J. Soulsby ½–with K. Baker & L. Smith	Halved
G. Stewart & J. Connachan lost to A. Benz & C. Hanlon	2 & 1

SINGLES (1):

McKenna lost to Benz	2 & 1
Connachan lost to Hanlon	5 & 4
Aitken lost to McDougall	2–holes
Robertson lost to Baker	7 & 6
Soulsby bt. Oliver	2–holes
Douglas lost to Inkster	7 & 6

FOURSOMES (2):

J. Connachan & W. Aitken lost to J. Inkster & C. Semple	3 & 2
K. Douglas & J. Soulsby lost to K. Baker & L. Smith	1–hole
M. McKenna & Mrs. Robertson bt. A. Benz and C. Hanlon	1–hole

SINGLES (2):

Douglas lost to Inkster	7 & 6
Stewart lost to Baker	4 & 3
Thomas lost to Oliver	5 & 4
Soulsby lost to McDougall	2 & 1
McKenna lost to Semple	1–hole
Robertson bt. Smith	5 & 3

RESULT: USA, 14½. GB & IRE, 3½.

1984 MUIRFIELD, SCOTLAND
CAPTAINS: DIANE BAILEY AND
PHYLLIS PREUSS

FOURSOMES (1):

C. Waite & B. New bt. J. Pacillo & A. Sander	2–holes
J. Thornhill & P. Grice ½–with L. Smith & J. Rosenthal	Halved
M. McKenna & L. Davies lost to M. Widman & H. Farr	1–hole

SINGLES (1):

Thornhill ½–with Pacillo	Halved
Waite lost to Hammel	4 & 2
Hourihane lost to Rosenthal	3 & 1
Thomas bt. Howe	2 & 1
Grice bt. Sander	2–holes
New lost to Widman	4 & 3

FOURSOMES (2):

C. Waite & B. New lost to L. Smith & J. Rosenthal	3 & 1
J. Thornhill & P. Grice bt. M. Widman & H. Farr	2 & 1
V. Thomas & C. Hourihane ½–with D. Howe & P. Hammel	Halved

Singles (2):

Thornhill lost to Pacillo	3 & 2
Davies bt. Sander	1–hole
Waite bt. Smith	5 & 4
Grice lost to Howe	2–holes
New lost to Farr	6 & 5
Hourihane bt. Hammel	2 & 1

RESULT: USA, 9½. GB & IRE, 8½.

1986 PRAIRIE DUNES, KANSAS
CAPTAINS: DIANE BAILEY AND JUDY BELL

FOURSOMES (1):

P. Johnson & K. Davies bt. D. Mochire & D. Ammaccapane	2 & 1
L. Behan & J. Thornhill bt. K. Kessler & C. Shreyer	7 & 6
B. Robertson & M. McKenna bt. K. Gardner & K. McCarthy	1–hole

SINGLES (1):

Johnson bt. Shannon	1–hole
Thornhill bt. Williams	4 & 3
Behan bt. Ammaccapane	4 & 3
Thomas lost to Kessler	3 & 2
Hourihane lost to Schreyer	2 & 1
Davies ½–with Mochrie	Halved

FOURSOMES (2):

P. Johnson & P. Davies bt. D. Mochrie & D. Ammaccapane	1–hole
L. Behan & J. Thornhill bt. L. Shannon & K. Williams	5 & 3
B. Robertson & M. McKenna ½–with K. Gardner & K. McCarthy	Halved

SINGLES (2):

Thornhill ½–with Shannon	Halved
Johnson bt. McCarthy	5 & 3
Behan lost to Gardner	1–hole
Thomas bt. Williams	4 & 3
Davies ½–with Kessler	Halved
Hourihane bt. Schreyer	5 & 3

RESULT: GB & IRE, 13. USA, 5.

INDEX

A

Aaron, Tommy, 78
Abbott, Lemuel, *14*
Adamson and Mcmurtrie, Messrs, 15
Albert, King of the Belgians, 32
Anderson, Jamie, 40, *40*, 42
Anderson, Willie, 44, *46*, *73*, 74
Apple Tree Gang, 13
Armour, Tommy, *29*, 94, *94*
Arthur, Duke of Connaught, 32
Auchterlonie, Willie, *21*
Augusta National Golf Club, 35, 48, 77, 90, *90*
Australia, *51*, 52

B

Douglas Bader Foundation tournament, *33*
bags, 20, *26*, 27
balata balls, 26
Balfour, Arthur James, *32*, 34
Ball, John, *41*, 42, 72
Ballesteros, Severiano, 58, *62*, 63, *63*, *76*, *76*, *85*
balls, *19*, 20, *21*, 23–7, 38, 44, 49
Barnes, Jim, 74, 75
Barton, Pamela, 65, *65*
Baudouin, King of the Belgians, 32
Behan, Lilian, 86
Belgian Amateur Championship, 32
Belgium, 8, 32
Berg, Patty, 66
Blackheath Common, London, 10–11
Brady, Mike, 74
Braid, James, 43–4, *43*, 46, 59, *83*
British Amateur Championship, *23*, 26, 42, 47, 48, *73*
British Open Championship, 26, 32, 39, 40, *40–1*, 42, 43, *44*, 46–7, *46*, 48, *48*, 49–50, 51–2, 54, 55, 57, 58, 63, 70, *71*, 72–3, *73*, 100
British Professional Matchplay, 43, 44, 49
British Women's Amateur Championship, 65, 67, 86
British Women's Championship, 64, 65
Burke, Jackie, 94

C

caddie-cars, *26*, 27
caddies, 27
Caird, Andrew, 34–5
Caird, Douglas, 34–5
cambuca, 10
Canada, 13
Canadian Ladies' Open Championship, 64
carbon-fibre shafts, 22
Carnoustie course, 58
Carrick, F & A, 19–20
Carter, Jo-Anne, 65, 66
Catherine of Aragon, Queen of England, 30
Charles I, King of England, 30
Charles II, King of England, 30
Chicago Golf Club, 13
Churchill, Winston Spencer, 34
Clark, Clive, 86
Claus, Prince of the Netherlands, 34
cleeks, 20
clothing, 27
clubs, 11–13, 90–8
clubs (equipment), *17–22*, 18–20, 22, *23*, 27, 44
Coe, Charlie, 78
Collet, Glenna, *64*, 65, 66
Constantine, King of Greece, 34
Cossar, Simon, 19
Cotton, Henry, 32, *48*, 49–50, *60*
course design, 13, 14, 15, 27, 77, 90–8
Crampton, Bruce, 76
Crawley, Leonard, 83
Crenshaw, Ben, 76, *76*, 79
Crosby, Bing, *51*
Curtis, Harriot, 86
Curtis, Margaret, 86
Curtis Cup, 86, *86*, 110–11
Cuyp, Aelbert, *8*

D

Daly, Fred, 48
Darwin, Bernard, 85
Davies, Karen, 86

Davies, Laura, 67
Demaret, Jimmy, 78
Dickson, Andrew, 18–19, 23
Dickson, John, 23–4
Diegel, Leo, 75
Dunlop 65 ball, 49
Dunn, Jamie, 38
Dunn, Willie, 13–14, 38
Dutch Open Championship, 34

E

Easterbrook, Syd, 82
Eclipse balls, 26
Edward VII, King of England, 31–2, *31*
Eisenhower, Dwight D, 35, *35*, 90
England, 10–11, 26
English Women's Championship, 64, 65
equipment, *17–27*
Espinho course, 14
Evans, Charles, 74

F

Fairlie, J O, 70
Faldo, Nick, *83*
Faulkner, Max, 48
Fazio, George, 51
feather balls, *19*, *21*, 23–4, *25*, 26, 38
Ferguson, Bob, *41*, 42
Fernie, Willie, *41*
Flower, Clement, *43*
Ford, Gerald, 35, *35*
Forestier, A, 31
Fowler, Frank, *12*
Fownes, William, 85
France, 8, 10
French Amateur Championship, 32
French Ladies' Open Championship, 64, 65, 67
French Open Championship, 43, 49
Fry, Sidney, 26

G

George V, King of England, 32, 34
George VI, King of England, 32
George, David Lloyd, 34–5
German Open Championship, 43
Jackie Gleason Classic tournament, 35
Gloucester Cathedral, 10, *12*
Goalby, Bob, *76*, 78
Goodman, Johnny, 74
Gourlay, Douglas, 20, 24
Gourlay, John, 26
Graham, David, 74, 76
graphite shafts, 22
Great Triumvirate, 43–4, *43–4*, 46, 74
Groom, Arthur, 15
Guldahl, Ralph, *72*, 74
gutta-percha balls *see* gutty balls
gutty balls, *21*, 22, 24–6, *25*, 38, 44

H

Hagen, Walter, *29*, 46–7, *47*, *59*, 75
Hardin, Hord, 77
Harmon, Claude, 94
Harris, Robert, 85
Haskell, Coburn, 26
Haskell balls, 26
Hassan, King of Morocco, 34
Havers, Arthur, 47
Herd, Alex (Sandy), 26, *26*
Hilton, Harold, 42, *42*, 72
history, *7–15*, 18–20, 22–7, 38–40, 42–4, 45–57
Hogan, Ben, 48, *48*, 51–2, 57, *60*, 74, 75
Holbrook, Harry, 13
Honourable Company of Edinburgh Golfers, 11, 19, 72, 96
Hope, Bob, *35*
Bob Hope Classic charity tournament, 35
Horsburgh, Thomas, 22
Hutchings, Charles, 26
Hutchinson, Horace, 22, 42, *42*,
Hutchison, Jock, 72, 75

I

Innes, William, *14*
Iran, Shah of, *33*, 34
Ireland, 14, 98, *98*
iron moulds, *25*, 26

J

Jacklin, Tony, 50, 74, 83, 85
James I, King of England, 10–11, 18, 23, 30

James II, King of England, 30–1
James II, King of Scotland, 8, 30
James III, King of Scotland, 30
James IV, King of Scotland, 30, *30*
Japan, 15
jeu de mail, 8, *8*, 10
Johnson, Patricia, 86
Jones Jr, Robert Tyre (Bobby), *29*, 32, *46*, 47–8, 57, *59*, 65, 72, *73*, 74, 75, 76, 77–8, 79, 85, 90, *90*, 92, 93, 94
Bobby Jones Award, 52, 67, 78

K

Kennedy, John Fitzgerald, *35*
Kish Island course, 34
Kobe Golf Club, 15

L

Lacoste, Catherine, *66*
Ladies' Professional Golf Association, 66
Lane, Bill, 77
Langer, Bernhard, *78*, 79, 85
Lees, Charles
On Musselburgh Links, *39*
Leopold, King of the Belgians, 32
Leitch, Cecilia, 64, *64*, 65
Lema, Tony, 53
Leopold, Prince of England, 32
Locke, Bobby, *51*, 52, *61*
Lockhart, Robert, 13, 26
Lopez, Nancy, *66*, 67
Lu, Liang Huan, *71*, 73
Lyle, Sandy, 85

M

McDermott, John J, 74
Macdonald, Charles Blair, 13, *15*
McEwan, Douglas, 20
McEwan, James, 19–20
McEwen, Peter, 19–20
McIntire, Barbara, *86*
MacKenzie, Alister, 77, 90, *90*
McNamara, Thomas, 74
Mangrum, Lloyd, 51
Marr, Dave, 94
Mary, Queen of Scots, 30, *31*
Massy, Arnaud, *71*, 72
Matheson, Thomas
'The Goff', 18
Maxwell, Robert, 72
Mayer, Dick, 94
Mayne, William, 23
Melvill, James, 23
Memphis Classic pro-am tournament, 35
Messieux, Simon, 23
Mill, Henry, 18–19
Miller, Johnny, 63
Mitchell-Innes, Gilbert, 40, 42
Mitchell-Innes, Norman, 42
Mize, Larry, 63, 79
Morris, Tom (Old), *19*, 24, 26, *37*, 38–9, *39*, 40, *59*
Morris, Tom (Young), 38, 39–40, 72, *59*
moulds, iron, *25*, 26
Mount Rokko course, 15
Muirfield course, 32, *48*, 49, 54, 72, 96–7, *96*

N

Nagle, Kel, 53, 72–3, 74
National Links, Long Island, 13
van der Neer, Aert, *7*
Negishi course, 15
Nelson, Byron, 48, 51, *51*, 52, *60*, 75, 78
Netherlands, 8
Newport Golf Club, 13
Nichols, Bobby, 76
Nicklaus, Jack, 47, 48, 53, *54*, 55, *55*, 57, 58, *62*, *73*, 74, *75*, 76, 78, *78*, 79, 83, 96–7, *96*
Nixon, Richard, *35*, 94
Norman, Greg, *69*, 70, 74, 76, 79, 94
North Berwick course, 38, *39*

O

Old Manchester Club, 11, 13
Oosterhuis, Peter, 34
Ouimet, Francis, 44, *44*, 74

P

paganica, 10, 18, 23
pall mall *see jeu de mail*

Palmer, Arnold, 35, *52*, 53–4, *61*, 73, 76, 78
Park, Willie, 38, 39, 40, *40*, 70
Park, Willie junior, 40, *40*, 42
Paterson, John, 30–1
Paterson, Robert Adam, 24–5
Pebble Beach course, *89*, 95, *95*
Philp, Hugh, *18*, 19, 20
Player, Gary, 48, 54–5, *54*, *61*, 74, 76, 78
politicians, 34–5
Portmarnock course, 98, *98*
Portugal, 14–15
Prestwick Golf Club, *12*, 38, 39, 42, 70, 72
Putnam, Kingman, 13
putters, 20, *23*

Q

Quebec Club, 13
Queen Adelaide Medal, 31

R

Rawlins, Horace, 13, 73, *73*
Ray, Ted, 44, *72*, 74
Reagan, Ronald, 35
Rees, Dai, 32
Reid, John, *12*, 13. 26
Rhondda Valley course, 32
Roberts, Clifford, 77
Robertson, Allan, 24, 25–6, 38, *39*, *59*
Robertson, Belle, 86, *86*
Rolls, Charles Stewart, 36
Rolls of Monmouth course, 34
Royal and Ancient Club of St Andrews, 11, 19, *19*, 20, *21*, 22, *23*, 26, *26*, 31–2, 38, 42, 44, 72, 85, 92
Royal Belfast Club, 14
Royal Birkdale course, 53, 54, 63, *71*, 73, 83
Royal Blackheath Golf Club, 11, 13
Royal Curragh Golf Club, 14
Royal Golf Club de Belgique, 32
Royal Liverpool Club, 26, 42, *71*, 85
Royal Lytham course, 11
Royal Melbourne Golf Club, 98, *98*
Royal Montreal Club, 13, 97, *97*
Royal Musselburgh Golf Club, 32, 38, *39*, *41*, 72
Royal North Devon Golf Club, 11, *12*, 42, 44
Royal Perth Golfing Society, 31
Royal St Georges Club, *26*, 43, 47, 49
Royal Wimbledon course, 32
royalty, *29*, 30–2, *30–1*, 34
rules, 11, 27
rut irons *see* track irons
Ryder, Samuel, 82, *83*
Ryder Cup, 44, *47*, 49, 50, 52, 54, 57, 63, *81*, 82–3, *83*, 102–5

S

St Andrews Club *see* Royal and Ancient Club of St Andrews
St Andrews Clubs of Yonkers, 13, *14*
St Andrews Old course, 92–3, *93*
St Andrews Royal Medal, 42
St Andrews Silver Medal, 42
St Cloud course, 32
Sandow, Robert, *33*, 34
Sands, Charles, 13
Santos course, 32
Sarazen, Gene, 48, *48*, 57, *60*, 65, 75, 78
scare-heading, 18
Schenectady putters, *23*
Scotland, 8, 10–11, 14, 20, 23
Shinnecock Hills Golf Club, 13, 14, *15*
shoes, 27
Shute, Densmore, 82
Simpson, George, 74
Simpson, Sir W G, 8
The Art of Golf, 8, *8*
Smart, John, 39
Smith, Alex, *73*, 74
Smith, Horton, 78
Smith, Macdonald, 74
Snead, Sam, 48, *48*, 51, 52, *60*, 75, 78
Sneed, Ed, 79
Society of St Andrews Golfers *see* Royal and Ancient Golf Club of St Andrews
Sota, Raymond, 63
Souchak, Mike, 94
South Africa, 52, 55
South African Open

Championship, 52, 54
Spanish Women's Open championship, 67
steel shafts, 22
Stranahan, Frank, 78
Strath, Davie, 40, 42
Strathclyde Golf Club, 58, *73*
Suggs, Louise, 66, *66*
Sunningdale courses, 42, *83*
surlyn balls, 26

T

Tallnadge, Henry O, 13
Taylor, John Henry, 42, 43–4, *43–4*, *59*, 72, 74, *83*
team events, 82–6
Tenby course, 14
Thomson, Peter, *51*, 52–3, *61*
Thornhill, Jill, 86
Tillinghast, AW, 94
Tokyo Club, 15
Tolley, Cyril, 85
Toronto Club, 13
tournaments, 71–86
track irons, 20, *21*
Travers, Jerome D, 74
Travis, Walter, *23*, 26, *26*
Trevino, Lee, *26*, 52, 57, *57*, 62, 73, 76
trolleys, 27
Troon Club, 19, 47, 48, 54
Tway, Bob, 76
two-piece balls, 26

U

United States, 8, 11, *12*, 13–14, 22, 26, 35, 44
United States Golf Association, 11, 14, 22, 26, 35, 74, 85
United States Masters Championship, 48, 51, 53, 54, 55, 57, 63, *63*, 70, *76*, 77–9, 100
United States National Amateur Championship, 13, *15*, 26, 42, 47, 48, 54, 55, 73, *73*, 74
United States Open Championship, 13, 44, 46, *46*, 47, 48, 51, 53, 54, 57, 58, 70, *72–3*, 73–4, 101
United States Professional Golf Association, 46, 51, 55, 57, 70, 75–6, *75*, 101
United States Women's Amateur Championship, *64*, 65, 66, 67
United States Women's Open Championship, 67
Upham, John, 13

V

Vardon, Harry, 42, 43–4, *43*, 44, *59*, 74, *83*
Vardon, Tom, 44
van de Velde, Adriaen
Golfers on the Ice near Haarlem, 8, *8*
de Vicenzo, Roberto, *76*, 78
Victoria, Queen of England, 31, 32, 97

W

Wales, 14
Walker, George Herbert, 85
Walker Cup, 48, *83*, 85–6, 106–9
Watson, Tom, 44, 57, *57*, 58, *62*, *73*, 76, 79
Weiskopf, Tom, 97
Western Open Championship, 57
Wethered, Joyce, 65, 72
Wethered, Roger, 72
White, Jack, 19–20
Whitworth, Kathy, *64*, 66
William IV, King of England, 31
Wilson, Robert, 19–20
Wilson Sporting Goods Co, 23
Windsor, Duchess of, *29*
Windsor, Duke of, *29*, 32
Winged Foot courses, 94, *94*, *95*
Wood, Adam, 19
Wood, Craig, 78, 94
Worplesdon Foursomes, 65
Wright, Mickey, 66
Wright & Ditson, *21*

Y

Yokoya course, 15

Z

Zaharias, Babe, 65, *65*
Zoeller, Fuzzy, 74, 79, 94